ON HUMANS

ON THE WAY THINGS ARE AND HOW HUMANS SCREWED IT UP

John L. Bowman

On Humans

Copyright 2019 John L. Bowman. All rights reserved.
Printed in the United States of America.
No part of this book may reproduced, stored in a retrieval system, or transmitted by any means without the written permission of the author.

ISBN 978-0-578-59973-1

Any people depicted in stock imagery are models, which are being used for illustrative purposes only. Because of the dynamic nature of the internet, any web addresses or links contained in this book may have changed since publication and may no longer be valid.
The views expressed in this work are solely those of the author.
This book was printed on acid-free paper.

I dedicate this book to all human free spirits

The cover is a portion of the *Golden Rule* painting by Norman Rockwell that was on the front page of the 1961 *Saturday Evening Post*. It features a gathering of men, women and children of different races, religions and ethnicities along with the golden rule to do unto others as you would have them do unto you.

I would like to thank my longtime trusted editor Kat Banks for designing this book.

CONTENTS

I   GOD'S OPENING REMARKS   1

II GOD'S COMMENTS ON THE NATURE
OF HUMANS INDIVIDUALLY   11

    The Nature of Emotions
    The Seven Deadly Sins
    The Nature of Desire
    The Nature of Happiness
    The Roles of Intuition and Reason
    The Nature of Will
    The Nature of Religion
    The Prioritization of Ideals
    The Nature of Wealth
    The Nature of Sexuality

III GOD'S REMARKS ON THE NATURE
OF HUMANS COLLECTIVELLY   55

    Freedom, Justice and Equality
    The Nature of Civilization
    The Relationship between the Individual and Society
    The Nature of Society
    The Nature of Relationships
    The Role of Government
    The Nature of the Law

    The Nature of Politics
    The Nature of Morality
    The Nature of Language
    Economics

IV GOD'S OBSERVATIONS ON HUMAN'S
    METAPHYSICAL SPECULATIONS   119

    The Nature of Knowledge
    The Difference between Reality and Illusion
    The Significance of Death
    The Nature of Truth
    Time and Space
    The Nature of Art
    Science
    Philosophy

V GOD'S CONCLUDING REMARKS   157

GOD'S OPENING REMARKS

Humans I am tired of your complaints. Constantly carping and whining, you blame me for your woes. You envision perfection, exclaiming that this must be the best of all worlds. When you conclude that it is not the best, you blame me for not creating it right. I found you interesting when you began to evolve, a kind of novelty, but your behavior has become tiresome. You are a latecomer in a much bigger picture, one that you intuitively understand but refuse to accept.

As hard as you may find this to believe, I did not create this world for you. You are only one small part of a whole. I had to design a vast, integrated universe that worked. It had to incorporate cause and effect, which requires limits. You came late, almost as an afterthought. You are but a tiny creature with limited understanding. I never intended to make this system the best or worst, a topic endlessly debated by your Mr. Leibniz and Mr. Voltaire. It just is. Most of your problems arise because you arrogantly think you are the center of my design. You keep trying to operate outside my patterns of nature and alter my unified system to your advantage. This effort causes most of your problems and very likely may cause your extinction.

That which I create I can take away.

I gave you only two instincts, the instinct to survive and the instinct to reproduce, period. Everything else that you do emanates from them. You are just an animal, like a bird, elephant, donkey, or dog. Your instincts are the same as those of all other animals on your puny planet, and you are not special. You are simple, easily explained, and very predictable. I designed you, like them, to live, reproduce, and then die. Your Mr. Rousseau had it only partially right: you are a beast but you are not noble. Your instincts to survive and reproduce manifest themselves in many ways, mainly self-interest. You are selfish. This defines you. It explains, as you will see, many of your problems.

It so happens that I gave you one advantage over your fellow animals—the ability to think and reason. It all started benignly. I just wanted you smart enough to crack open nuts with a rock. I gave you these qualities only as an afterthought. I gave the other animals defenses such as claws, speed, or camouflage to enhance their instincts to survive. You were naked and originally dull. So, I gave you a little cleverness so you could compete in the survival game. However, you so extensively developed this quality that you now exercise more control over your environment than I originally envisioned. You have also commenced wondering and forever projecting your metaphysical imagination onto your circumstances. This has been a curse and blessing. A curse because you now need purpose and meaning in life, something I never intended, and a blessing for many because you now can thwart, in a limited way, my original design. This meddling with my design, when done to extreme, is causing you many woes. What I like least about this new development is that it has made you a complaining little shit.

Let me tell you what reality is so you might appreciate how much you have screwed it up. As I have said, I intended an animal that would survive and reproduce. I gave you certain qualities to enhance your survivability. Your body, for example, grasps with hands, chews with teeth, heals itself, has legs so it can move about, and was originally covered with hair for warmth. There are many other qualities I will not go into. I also gave you aggressiveness so that you can create and destroy. You aggressively create shelter and search for food. You also aggressively defend yourself from whatever threatens your survival, such as other animals and people. I also instilled in you the urge to reproduce. You inherently seek the opposite sex, experiencing great pleasure in coition and love to maintain the bond necessary for procuring and raising offspring. Your instincts are just like those of all the other animals. You are aggressive and selfish to survive and reproduce. Pretty simple so far.

You found that surviving is easier when you aggregate. This development has raised myriad problems for you. Let me tell you what I originally envisioned. I planned for only small units of humans, usually families consisting of fathers, mothers, and children. They would have a hierarchy based on strengths and weaknesses; one would procure and protect and the other birth nurture. These small units would interact with other small units or clans and cooperate to survive and perpetuate your species. When these units cooperated with each other your communities naturally developed which was all part of my plan. What spontaneously arose was an organic morality that helped you all get along. This morality stems from your survival instinct, and your self-interest drives it. For example, you agreed among yourselves not to kill, steal, or lie to avoid being killed, stolen from, or lied to. Your Mr. Hobbes accurately explained this system when he described social contracts. The idea was that each individual would voluntarily agree with other individuals to limit their actions. Each agreed to limit their freedom in exchange for a little security. This is what I intended, and you call it morality. The system spontaneously arose because you aggregated.

You call this moral system many things but it is nothing more than a pattern. There are other patterns, including physical patterns, social patterns, and instinctual patterns. Your see them everywhere. The physical patterns are things such as night and day, birth, life and death, and the seasons. The social patterns are the many predictable forms of relations and associations that come about when you aggregate. The instinctual patterns are what you call human nature. They are neither good nor bad, they just are. Nature is a pattern and I am a pattern. Everything is a pattern of nature. You usually screw up when you attempt to alter these timeless, universal, unalterable, and preordained patterns.

More often than not, you cleverly aided these patterns. In your system of morality, for example, you began calling human qualities that support this pattern "virtues" and those that do not "vices." When a man is peaceful, honest, and trustworthy, you call him virtuous. When he kills, steals, and lies, you call him virtueless. Your virtues support the natural moral pattern. Along with morality, you also devised the concept of integrity, a quality that causes you to adhere to the principles of this natural moral pattern. Those with virtue are said to be principled, which sometimes requires you to act contrary to your instincts and desires. You also conceived the ideas of good and evil. Virtues that support this natural system, you call good. Virtues that disagree with the system, you call evil.

You also invented the word justice, a very curious word, to denote the result of this natural system of morality. What is fair and right is just. You created these concepts—virtue, vice, integrity, good, evil, and justice—to support morality, and they do. You are a crafty little shit. They also allowed you to develop your civilizations because, as one of your thinkers said, every liberty each of you enjoys depends on another restraining himself. Your civilizations, and the civil liberties they bring would be impossible without you restraining your instincts. This self-restraint, based on self-interest, comes from these concepts that you conceived. I did not dream them up, you did. I just created the patterns and you gave them names.

Because of your selfishness and drive to survive, you are inherently competitive. You compete to survive and perpetuate yourself. You compete for sustenance and mates. This makes you naturally aggressive. But you are also capable of cooperation when it helps you survive. You cooperate in morality, civilizations, and economics when it is in your best interests. But, as you will see, you often do it selectively.

An economic pattern naturally and spontaneously evolved. It consisted of markets, bartering, negotiations, and exchanging. Your great economist Adam Smith best described this system. It was a natural outgrowth of your instinct to survive and selfish nature. You call it mercantilism or sometimes capitalism. I supposed that if you were to be naturally selfish souls, then the best system to create wealth should harness this reality. Much to my surprise, your selfish and egoistic natures caused you to work like dogs to further your individual interests. This economic system balanced supply and demand, allocated scarce resources, increased production of the things you want and need, and kept your population under control. Competition ruthlessly superintends it as a great equalizer.

Your wonderfully conceived system works better than I thought it would. The complex interplay of economic self-interests helps the health and wealth of your communities, which increases your chances of surviving as a species. Mr. Smith called it an "invisible hand."

The problem is you have totally screwed up all this. I have watched with both wonderment and dismay at your endless efforts to change the natural order of things. Your problems arise from many sources but usually when you upset these patterns. You have come up with some fantastic ideas, concepts, and schemes. You have created a virtual other world of ideas that have nothing to do with what I created. They are so unrelated to the patterns of nature that I, God, often have difficulty relating to what you think and what you are. You have created complicated artificial constructs like societies, states, and civilizations. You have conceived of religions, language, and things like human law. You have also, in the process, conceived of concepts like justice, truth, and art. Your mind is one busy little bee.

Let me digress briefly and explain my use of the word "construct" because I use it often. Constructs are empty abstractions of yours that you endeavor to make concrete. You make these arrangements from your imagination. They are very much like constructing one of your buildings. You first conceive of a structure, then design it, and finally build it. Your mind brings together the components to create a structure that does not exist in nature. Your imaginary constructs include things like government, religion, and law. They have become a significant source of your difficulties. They often make you your own worst enemy.

To carry this point further, I want you to think of your lives as waffles. These imaginary and artificial constructs, entities that exist only in your mind, are metaphorical waffle irons imposed on your human natures, which are like free and fluid waffle batter. Your lives get stamped and become like a waffle. You make yourselves conform with obligations, duties, and responsibilities. Unfortunately, your waffle irons make a mess while making waffles. Most of my comments address the mess you make.

Your clever mind and fertile imagination created this mess, and it has led you into some agonizingly curious and empty contradictions. In fact, because of your imagination you are a walking contradiction and virtual living irony. Take for example your wonderment over nature vs. nurture. Originally you had it right, you thought you were nature. Then some of you began claiming that you were also the product of nurturing, that other things were responsible for what you are. I have news for you: they are the same. Nature is nurture and nurture is nature. They are all part of one pattern. You are born with certain predispositions, but what makes you what you are also includes external patterns that are preordained and natural. Combined, they are nature and you are the result.

Now do not get me wrong. You have some free will. I so enjoyed many of your early religious thinkers' thoughts about this topic you call determinism vs. free will-Mr. Aquinas stands out. The answer is that you live in a determined universe with determined patterns but have some control over which course to take. Your recent philosophers call this compatabilism in which free will is the ability to act according to your motives without arbitrary hindrance from other people or institutions and determinism is when you have no control over events like your death. Put from my perspective, I know the future and you can fiddle a little with your affairs. In the big picture, however everything is cause and effect but you do not see it. What happens, which course you choose, what pattern applies, all have inexorable, innumerable, and necessary consequences. Your Mr. Pope was a great poet but a lousy thinker. He thought what is, is right because it is the best, but he was wrong. On the contrary, what is, is right only because it is correct, which means that you have some capacity to improve things. This comes about mostly through the proper application of your clever imagination and ability to reason. I applaud this and intended it to an extent. But you surprised me when you began using these qualities to confound my original plans and stray too far from my original patterns.

Before I begin let me clear up a few things. First, your Mr. Lucretius was right, nothing does come from nothing. Mr. Pope was right in that you are but part of one large chain of being. Mr. Spinoza, one of your better speculators, was right when he said whatever is, is in me and nothing can either be or be conceived without me. He is the one, by the way, who told you that I am nature. Also, tell that irritating Mr. Hume that cause and effect is more than habit. So now, let us examine some of your world in light of this explanation of the way things are. I have a lot to say, so for simplicity let me discuss your transgressions individually first, then collectively, and finally metaphysical.

II

GOD'S COMMENTS ON THE NATURE OF HUMANS INDIVIDUALLY

You may not believe me, but you are an animal with the same vestigial instincts as other animals. However, your cleverness causes you to think differently, which makes you a different kind of animal. For example, you misinterpret your emotions, construct wrongful states of feeling, and believe things that do not exist. Your clever imagination increasingly defines you, which is gradually causing you to be what you are not. The result: you have become a frustrated, ignoble, neurotic, and mildly schizophrenic extra-human something.

The Nature of Emotions

You have so twisted and rearranged your emotions that even I have a hard time understanding what you are doing. You have completely lost touch with their original purpose. You create fantastic schemes to explain and justify them, innumerable variations on the same emotion, and such subtle shades of feeling that you now live in an emotional world that confounds you. Take for example your word ennui which is a rich person's boredom due to idleness. None of the other animals need such a word because none are rich, idle or bored. You have invented a nonsense word to describe a state of emotion only you suffer from due to your constructs.

Let me give it to you straight: your emotions derive from only two sources, the instincts to survive and reproduce. All your emotions emanate from these instincts, meaning they are based on self-interest. You have the same emotional instincts as all other animals and you are not different or special. The only difference is that you are clever, a clever dog.

You have five basic emotional instincts. They are love, hate, fear, jealousy, and anger. Dogs have these five too but are not smart enough to give them names. They just experience them. Dogs do not write literature or describe sublimity. Think about it, dogs are affectionate and gentle when they court and mate. They do so because it enables them to reproduce. It lets them perpetuate their species. You call this love. Dogs are forever vigilant and ready to pounce on their enemies, which allow them to thwart that which threatens their survival and ability to reproduce. You call this hate. When physically threatened they will either fight or flee, instincts that enhance their chances of survival. Fleeing you call fear and fight you call anger. Finally, when some other dog has the bone they want or the mate they desire, they try to take them away, something you call jealousy. All these instincts, which you call emotions, are based on self-interest. You are nothing more than a thinking dog.

Down deep you know that each of these basic emotions enhances your survival and ability to reproduce. You know intuitively that each is based on your self-interest. For example, you often say that you must love yourself before you can love someone else because if you do not, you will not think yourself worthy enough to give or receive love. Loving, therefore, also stems from self-interest. You also say giving makes you feel good, which makes giving an inherently selfish action. You hate because you feel diminished. You fear so you can live to fight another day. You get angry because you have been injured in some way, and you feel jealousy because you want what someone else has. These are the essential origins of your emotions. But now it gets complex because your philosophers, and especially the so-called literati, have confused matters.

You create innumerable dispositions and subtle feelings from each of these basic emotions. From love you get elation, pleasure, compassion, tenderness, empathy, gentleness, concupiscence, forgiveness, lust, mercy, happiness, and mirth. From hate you get vengeance, violence, deception, fury, and often one very bad temper. From fear you get surprise, suffering, aggression, anxiety, miserliness, and prudence. From anger you get determination, resentment, and cruelty. Finally, from jealousy you derive competitiveness, avarice, and envy. There are so many more derivations that it is impossible to describe them in detail. Besides, you probably would not understand my explanation. Instead, let me describe some strange consequences of your misapplication and misunderstanding of these basic emotions—consequences that derive primarily from your runaway imagination.

You extend love to mean love your neighbor, enemy, and even humankind. You now find yourself loving those who endeavor to extinguish you. You also have universalized hate, so now some hate everything in the forms of misanthropy, misogamy, and misogyny, along with a host of other words beginning with "mis." You often hate that which helps you. You now fear the unknown, others, and even yourself. You fear what you do not understand, which is a lot, and people who are unlike you, and they are many. You fear for unsupportable and imaginary reasons. Your anger often becomes so chronic that any perturbance triggers it. Thus, you often find yourself angry for little or no reason. And anything that diminishes you incites jealously. You are often jealous just because you desire something someone else has, whether you need it or not. You have become not only a thinking dog, but a schizophrenic one as well.

Just so you understand, a few emotions emanate from your circumstances. They are better described as states. For example, when nothing threatens your survival and ability to reproduce, you experience equanimity, peace, tranquility, boredom, laziness, and apathy. These temporary states occur when other basic emotions are not needed. (Those French people are the masters of emotional nomenclature.) When your survival or reproduction is at stake, you experience sadness, depression, or melancholy; when they are being enhanced, you experience honor, awe, zeal, élan, and hope. The appreciation of art, for example, is a form of awe, which is a very strange and convoluted extension of this state. Also, a few manifestations of these emotions occur because of what you call civilization, though I did not plan them. These include guilt, modesty, and shame. They arose to enforce the need for individuals to survive within your communities. I will discuss them later.

One last emotional state permeates everything. It derives from your original instincts and their natural consequence, which is self-interest. It lurks behind every one of these emotions, explains many of your actions, permeates your societies, adulterates your relationships, and may cause your extinction. It is the state of pride. You think you are special, unique, and especially worthy. You think everything that happens, happens only to you. You think you are the center of the world because you are concerned only with your survival and your ability to reproduce. You see this emotional state manifest everywhere. It comes in the forms of vanity, arrogance, egoism, haughtiness, and superciliousness. To my great displeasure, when your pride becomes extreme, you think you are me. Your pride becomes hubris. When your puny little pride has been injured, you experience indignation, insult, and contempt, and you react with insolence, disgust, and umbrage. Your sense of pride is out of control, you are not special, and you look foolish when your pride gets the best of you.

Pride, by the way, creates your misanthropes. They forever object to pernicious human characteristics that pride causes. For your Mr. Juvenal, the objection was blind desire, for Mr. Machiavelli it was the loss of virtue, for Mr. Rochefoucauld it was self interest and egoism (he thought vanity drove your very being), for Mr. Molière it was your arrogance, for Mr. Swift it was your base passions and lack of rationality (he called you Yahoos), and for Mr. Mencken it was your pretentiousness. As your Mr. Plato pointed out long ago, pride is why you diminish others of your kind. This diminishment causes much of your suffering.

The Seven Deadly Sins

Let me go into a little more detail on a few these emotions for your edification. Originally, you were part of nature's pattern. You were kind of stuck in it. This pattern mitigated your emotional excesses through the combination of competition with nature and other animals. These superintended your emotions and desires. Scarcity was the rule, not the exception. For example, you could feel rapacious without being greedy because there was not much to take. But you are a clever little shit, having largely managed to extract yourself from this pattern. The original emotions enabled you to survive and reproduce within the pattern but did not change when you escaped. They subsequently became unnecessary and destructive excesses. You just kept running with them, seeing where they would take you, so to speak. The consequences are what some in your little world call sins. I really dislike the word "sin" because your religious seers devised it to instill guilt-it just carries too much baggage. They are not really sins but rather the excess of normal emotions. They are predictable and rooted in your self-interest.

To better understand these sins and put them in perspective, I will describe their consequences. There are a lot of them but you only admit to seven. They are pride, envy, anger, lust, gluttony, avarice, and sloth. We have already discussed some. Pride detaches you from reality and is the source of other sins including envy, anger, and avarice. You say that pride goeth before the fall and the humble among you rarely suffer a fall from this sin. You are right: he who expects little is rarely disappointed. Envy is just extreme jealousy, and anger is indeed ugly when it becomes rage. Lust is entirely normal and instinctual but you have made it an end in itself in your pursuit of sensual pleasure. Gluttony is excessive consumption, especially of food. You once ate as much food as you could to survive. Now you eat for the sake of eating and get fat, sick, and grotesque. Avarice is greed that originates in jealousy and envy. You now hoard far more than you need to survive. Finally, sloth was once your need to rest and conserve energy. Now some of you rest all the time. Your Mr. Voltaire once said that work keeps you from the three great evils of vice, boredom, and poverty. Now, with sloth, many of your kind embody these evils. These are your most conspicuously excessive emotions because your passions and feelings drive you, unencumbered by reason and willpower.

Many of you have become prisoners of your passions. Your strange Mr. Rochefoucauld once said that vices bring about your greatest misfortunes. He was right because indulging in these sins causes you to live unhappy lives. Some of you always feel deprived of things you think you are entitled to. I have news for you: the patterns of nature do not come with entitlements.

I am not expressing my views to preach but to edify. What I have done is done and only you can improve your emotional circumstances. I hold little hope that you will learn from me because you are so driven by your emotions and so unwilling to think. Despite this, I will give you a hint about how to control your sins. It comes from your eminent and ancient Mr. Aristotle who long ago conceived a way to govern these excessive passions. He called it the Doctrine of the Mean, which teaches avoiding extremes. His theory is important for you because your emotional extremes cause you the most problems. Courage, for example, is the mean and is good, whereas foolhardiness and rashness on one end and cowardice and timidity on the other are the bad extremes. The antidote is temperance and moderation, which steer you clear of emotional extremes. Otherwise, go with the flow, indulge yourselves, and live your lives in unhappy dog-like angst.

The Nature of Desire

Now, humans, let us talk about what drives your emotions, causes the seven sins, and makes you live in this unhappy angst. It is desire, and you are a desire machine. The things you want and lack of appreciation for what you have forever amazes me. You are never satisfied and you perpetually desire. Desires are not the same as emotions; rather they are what drive them. They are the extent or degree of your want and they determine the intensity of your emotions. Your desires are not inherently wrong; they are entirely natural. I gave them to you to succor your chances of survival and reproduction, and they worked pretty well. You were forever scavenging for food, shelter, and mates. I intended for you to use these desires within the patterns as a motivator. I had found that animals without this motivation, the ones who were always satisfied, had a way of dying out.

The problem is that you have partially escaped the patterns of nature and obtained the original objects of your desire, but your desire remains. Therefore, the problem is no longer the object of want but rather desire itself. You now desire for desire's sake. You desire what you cannot have, what you do not have, and what you do not need. Now you even desire things you do not want, a state of affairs you call irony.

Watching you is so curious because when you have achieved one desire, it dissipates and you begin to desire something else. Desire is like a mirage for you: what you want is always somewhere else and not where you are. And when you reach the mirage, it has moved. So you begin to desire another mirage. Your Mr. Juvenal and Mr. Johnson best described this problem, calling it the vanity of human wishes. Your problem has become the state of desire itself. You are perpetually wishing for what you do not have. You are suspended in a never-ending state of want. You are, as your Mr. Swift so imaginatively described, a Yahoo.

Your desires are many. The most obvious and pedestrian ones are for wealth, power, and prestige. You are forever scurrying around seeking more gold, more influence, and more honors. You also are driven to experience sensual pleasure. For example, you engage in sex more for entertainment than procreation. Because your basic needs mostly have been met, you desire objects that are more esoteric. So now you want abstract and ethereal concepts like happiness, pleasure, and knowledge. They are the consequences of your new ungrounded, free-floating, and highly generalized desires. Historically, these esoteric states just happened; you did not pursue them. You were happy when you were satiated and warm, you were felicitous when you had satisfied your sexual appetite, and you felt knowledgeable when you knew how to get your next meal. You experienced these feelings in response to some event. Now you seek out these feelings for the sake of having them.

Watching your thinkers grapple with this situation is fascinating. They are intuitive enough to understand the problem of desire but cannot agree on the solution. Your Mr. Plato was among the first to see desire as the central reason for your unhappiness. He thought the solution was to have the right desire, or natural desires. Mr. Aristotle, as I mentioned, thought it was a matter of moderating your desires. He thought prudence was the answer. Many of your thinkers, like the stoic Mr. Aurelius, believed that use of reasoning could limit your desires. My personal favorite comes from the Epicureans, led by your hedonist Mr. Epicurus. He said the way to solve desire is to satiate it. For this group, pleasure was the greatest good. Your Mr. Boethius called this situation the Wheel of Fortune, a wheel that goes round and round but never gets anywhere. For him the solution was simple: do not get on it, and if you already have, get off. I do not have any solutions for you because, after all, you are what you are. All I can say is that you are victim of your own cleverness.

The Nature of Happiness

In light of my comments about desire, the nature of what you call happiness now should be obvious even to you. Happiness is among those free-floating concepts you have devised. It was your idea, not mine. You always whine about not being happy and blame me. All I ever intended for you were occasional feelings of pleasure associated with the fulfillment of your instincts. Your Mr. Johnson was correct when he observed that brief interludes of happiness make endurable your otherwise painful lives. You have inflated these intervals into a source of meaning and purpose in your lives, thoroughly confusing yourselves. You now believe that happiness is a real, achievable, and enduring state. The irony (I love that concept of yours) is that you torment yourself into a state of unhappiness because you so desire happiness, something you can never obtain. You think you should be happy so you are forever pursuing that goal, and when you are not happy, it makes you unhappy. You backed yourself into a corner on this one.

Let me make this clear. What if I gave dogs your cleverness and gave you their teeth and claws? Dogs would begin thinking about the concept of happiness and pursuing what makes them happy. They would agree among themselves that no dog take another's bone, none fight, and all have unlimited sex—a virtual dog heaven on earth. So they would create a dog legislature to enact dog laws that further these goals, and a dog police force made up of German shepherds to enforce them. Pious poodles then would begin agitating to limit sexual activity in the name of dog morality, but because puppy childhoods are so short, most dogs would demand institutionalized promiscuity. Then the dog literati would begin to write doggerel and clichés as if it is a dog's world and everything is going to the dogs. (Sorry, I so enjoy your sense of humor I got carried away.)

The point is this: in your cleverness you created the concept of happiness that you so desire, as well as the flawed constructs to achieve it. The other animals are not clever like you and have no comparable concept, so they do not worry about being unhappy. Human happiness is an illusion. You are not only a thinking, schizophrenic dog, but a delusional one as well.

Your Mr. Mill had it right when he described happiness as the presence of pleasure and absence of pain. The consequences are self-evident, at least to me. Despite your longings, you are incapable of ever achieving a state of complete happiness. I did not design reality for your happiness, I never intended you to be what you call happy, and I bat last. Your little lives are essentially one of toil, discouragement, disappointment, pain, angst, and struggle interspersed with occasional bouts of pleasure. You are, as your Mr. Freud so intuitively understood, necessarily and constitutionally incapable of happiness for two reasons. The first is obvious: you are consigned to suffering by nature. You have little control over what nature offers you, including what happens to your bodies. Your Mr. Hobbes, for example, described your lives in the state of nature as solitary, poor, nasty, brutish, and short. Second, your associations and relations forever thwart you. Your constructs of families, states, and civilizations are built on the renunciation of your instincts. They limit your freedoms, especially your sexual freedoms, impart responsibilities, and repress your aggressive nature. They engender in you conscience, which causes you to feel guilty. Dogs do not feel guilty, only you do.

If you doubt me, and I am sure you do, consider what lengths you go to experience pleasure and avoid pain. You do it chemically through drugs like alcohol. This does not bring happiness, only hangovers and death (and closer to me) if carried to extremes. You endeavor to modify your instincts. Your stoics as well as some of your Eastern religions, like Buddhism for example, try to kill them. This method does not make you happy and only creates quietness. Others, such as your Epicureans, preach the pursuit of your instinctual sensual pleasures to achieve happiness. This only brings momentary and fleeting pleasure interspersed with long periods of anguish spent searching for the next sensual pleasure. Some of you sublimate proclivities and heighten others to achieve happiness. Your artists and intellectuals commonly do this. But this does not make you happy; it only results in mild gratification that few can experience. Many create illusions and live in dream worlds, like many of your art aficionados and religious zealots. But this does not bring happiness because some are less imaginative, and those who are know that down deep their illusions are false.

A surprising number of you limit reality's influence and become delusional. When an individual does this, you call them a hermit, and when many do it together, you call them religious. But this does not work because reality is too strong. Some intrepid souls persist in pursuing happiness through love. These are your hopeless romantics. But they fail because when love is lost they experience what is probably your greatest unhappiness. Finally, there are those among you who fight unhappiness with neurotic illness. You think they are crazy, but my advice is do not knock it until you have tried it.

As the bearer of bad news, I suppose I should be sorry. But I am just telling you the way it is.

Let us conclude this part of my observations on a positive note and see if you can learn a few lessons from all this. Your concept of happiness does not exist, and you should only expect and be satisfied with temporary bouts of pleasure. Pleasure is felt, not intellectualized. Grand schemes, like that of your screwy Mr. Bentham who preaches happiness for the most, do not bring happiness.

Theories, ideologies, and concepts are not what make you happy. True pleasure comes from small things in incremental steps. Thinking cannot make you happy, but you can do the things that make you happy and one day realize you feel less pain. Only you can make yourself what you call happy. I offer only temporary bouts of pleasure and occasional relief from pain. The essence of happiness is simplicity because satisfying your simple instinctual desires brings temporary bouts of pleasure. Indeed, your Mr. Thoreau, the cabin builder, once admonished you to simplify, simplify, simplify. And finally, keep in mind what your ancient Mr. Erasmus once said: no man is happy until he dies; until then he is only lucky.

The Roles of Intuition and Reason

Before we get too far into my opinions of humans I want to explain intuition and reason because they affect so much of what you do and think. They profoundly influence things such as the expression of your instinctual emotions, your strongest desires, what brings you pleasure, and how you associate and interact with others. They virtually determine the form of many of your civilizing constructs. These include your families, communities and states. Intuition and reason are the lenses through which you perceive reality and consequently color your worldview. Your problem is that you use them capriciously, interchangeably, selfishly, and wrongly. You often use reason to justify some intuitive belief and intuition to modify some reasonable conclusion. Your thinkers endlessly debate the relative merits of these cognitive processes. Some think intuition is best and others reason. They have developed so many lofty theories about which is superior that you have, as usual, thoroughly confused what I intended.

I gave both to you, they are natural, and they have advantages and disadvantages.

They are just ways of thinking and different methods for making decisions. Intuition is more vestigial, primitive, and atavistic. It derives from your primary emotions of love, hate, fear, jealousy, and anger. Intuition is the source of your spirituality and a more instinctual way of thinking. For example, you intuitively flee with fear, fight with anger, and reproduce without thinking. You use most of your passions and feelings in intuitive thinking. Intuition is natural, needed, and in you. It is closest to your essential human natures.

Reason is different. You took my gift of cleverness and developed reason. This long and difficult but natural process enhanced your survivability. Your higher faculty of reason distinguishes you from the other animals. It flourished because you pondered, evaluated, wondered, and speculated. While not necessarily conflicting with your emotions, it often superintends and controls them. Your David Hume was only partially right. Your reason is natural, needed and in you.

Here is where it gets interesting. You mix up reasoning and intuition so much that you get confusing consequences and unreliable answers. Most of you cannot even tell the difference. First, it is easier to be intuitive than rational. Intuition comes naturally and reason takes work.

Your Mr. Emerson said that most of you do not think because it is so hard. Intuitive thinking usually results in better decisions for you individually because it draws on more premises. When you make decisions with intuition you unwittingly tap the vast reservoir of your experiences which surfaces more premises. However, your intuitive premises are occasionally wrong—they may not apply to the decision at hand, or your self-interests sometimes overly influence them. Intuitive thinking, when taken to extremes, often results in passion, lynch mobs and murder. It is the primary cause of all the sins discussed earlier. It also sometimes impedes your relationships and associations.

Your reason creates civilizations, mitigates intuition's excesses and occasionally proscribes your egoistic inclinations. You use it to develop concepts like justice. Indeed, you call reasonable individuals "just." But reason often draws on too few premises and, as with intuition, sometimes-faulty premises. Thus, reason sometimes produces very unrealistic and far-fetched ideas and solutions. Many of your thinkers, such as Mr. Kant and Mr. Burke, explained this defect. Mr. Kant disliked many of your ungrounded metaphysical assertions and Mr. Burke believed that political ideologies derived from abstract reasoning produced wrong ways to govern. Your unchecked reason sometimes creates detached, free-floating and unnatural beliefs and ideas. In its worst and most extreme form reason drives many of your millenary thinkers like Mr. Marx and Mr. Lenin whose means too often resulted in heinous crimes committed at the altar of their unrealistic, and ostensibly reasonable, ends. Reason usually initiates your metaphysical speculations, takes you furthest from your essential human natures,and detaches you from my patterns.

Now I will talk briefly on one touchy subject. First, though, let me say that I love men and women equally. Both are natural, needed and different. Genders think differently. Each complains that they do not understand the other. Many reasons explain this but mainly it is because men tend to use reason more and women intuition. I intended it this way. Men, the procurers, needed to know how to crack nuts and hunt and women needed to divine children's needs to perpetuate your species. Both are natural and within nature's patterns but problematic when extended beyond the patterns. Within the patterns they succor your survivability and ability to reproduce. Outside the patterns, men's reason too often leads to some very bad ideas while women's intuition creates runaway passions.

What both need to know is that these two different ways of thinking are not necessarily at odds but rather complementary when used properly. Intuition is good when you need to draw on your experiences, particularly when making personal decisions. Reason is good when you need to organize and judge personal experiences, especially when making collective decisions. They are like one of your ships with its officers and enlisted corps. The intuitive sailors run the ship and the reasoned officers guide it. The sailors make the ship work and the officers give it discipline and direction. Both are needed and without each other the ship would be a rudderless ship of fools.

Let me give you one more prosaic example before we leave this topic. Today, you do what you call buying a place to live, a house in your words. If you use only intuition when choosing a house you might end up making a purchase you regret. For example, you might forget to consider that you need three bedrooms for your three children or you might forget that because you work downtown you needed to live within five miles of the city center. If you use only reason, you might forget to ask yourself whether it feels like home because you focused only on the need for three bedrooms and convenience to downtown.

Innumerable things tucked into your memory but out of view come to fore when you intuitively decide about your house. For example, with intuition you would notice the traffic noise that you so dislike. In the first case, you bought a house with too few bedrooms and a very long commute and in the other you bought a house that does not feel like home due to the traffic noise. The better solution would have been to first establish your reasonable parameters, find the house and then ask yourself if it intuitively feels right to you. The point is this: use both intuition and reason, and use them properly.

The Nature of Will

Your will is hard to explain because it is such an invisible attribute. It is like describing yellow. You never define it but rather characterize its qualities. You call it cheerful, pleasant, or bright, but these are not yellow's essence.

Like your will, yellow simply cannot be further reduced, deduced, or comprehensively explained. I cannot explain will in terms you can comprehend because of your limited ability to understand. Your knowledge has limits, but that is another topic.

I could describe will as your essence or your being, but these terms just beg further explanation. Many of your thinkers have tried to describe will but failed. Some thought of it as a rational and universal force that motivates or compels, some as a mental faculty that causes you to act upon what the will itself has chosen, some the collective voice of the people, and a few as what approves or disapproves of your choices and desires. Most of you would agree that your will is what initiates and has the power to control and determine your actions. It controls your desires and intentions. Most would also agree that will involves choosing, volition, intention, and the ability to make yourself do something. It is what moves the unmoved to action. Will encompasses all these but more.

Your will is everything and without it you are nothing. You must have a will to live. Will makes you get up in the morning, makes you go to work, makes you eat, makes you love, and propels you to achieve goals. It depresses me to see so many of you wasting your lives thinking you should do something and never doing it. These people spend their lives in a state of velleity, an inert state of forever wishing without will. Many, for example, decide to defer doing what they want until they retire, but when they retire they are too old do what they want. Your Mr. Sophocles said waiting to the evening to see the splendor of the day is a mistake.

If you do not act upon what you feel and think, then feeling and thinking are passive and pointless states. All your emotional attributes are pointless unless your will engages them.

In essence, your will is your instinct to survive—you call it the will to live. I gave will to you and the other animals because I wanted you to survive. It is among your most essential and primal attributes, and without it you would perish. Those with the greatest will survive the best and reproduce the most. Collaterally, in your modern societies, those with the strongest wills tend to accomplish the most and be the most successful. Those without it you call lazy, languid, slothful, and indolent. Your will is a wonder and works great when used properly.

Your will is neither good nor bad. It can be naturally constructive or destructive. For example, the constructive will enhances your survival and reproduction by compelling you to seek food or a mate. It also is necessary to maintain your various constructs such as families, states, and civilization. These constructs would be impossible without will. You must have the will, or be willing, to adhere to virtues and ethics that support these constructs, and you must be willing to limit you instincts to live in peace. Your societal constructs would not function without your will for precisely these reasons. Your will also can be destructive when your survival is threatened. For example, you must have the will to destroy what endangers you.

Your problems begin when you take your will out of the natural patterns and misapply and misinterpret it. You have begun to extend your will outside the patterns, causing some crazy consequences. Your will has become a free-floating entity far beyond the simple will to survive. You have created a vigilant and ever-present willfulness to maintain and navigate you constructs.

The application of your will outside the patterns of nature has had many consequences, and the worst is your wanton destructiveness. You see it everywhere in your societies today. The most obvious is war, which I will discuss shortly. Not so obvious is the extension of your will to survive to the will for everyone to survive, a sentiment embodied in your Mr. Blanc's admonition "to each his need." This appears constructive but has created a huge needy and dependent population and overpopulation. This manifestation of your willfulness is destroying your environment and, ironically, challenging your very ability to survive.

To complicate matters, because you are operating outside the patterns, you also have devalued your will. You forever amaze me because you take this primal quality called will, make it valuable, debate its merit, forget where it came from, and then proceed to devalue it. You think other things control you beyond your will and blame the patterns themselves for your misfortunes rather than your lack of willpower. For example, you say that crime and poverty are societies' fault and not the criminals or the poor. This strange misunderstanding ignores the importance of will. First, it devalues the individual's willingness to adhere to the ethics that sustain your constructs like civilization, and second it devalues the individual's willingness to work. Your innocent misapplication of will has become counterproductive.

Some of you have taken this misapplication to sinister extremes. Two of your craziest thinkers come to mind, Mr. Schopenhauer and Mr. Nietzsche. They took your will and twisted it into the will to destroy. Mr. Schopenhauer misconstrued your will to survive as an aggressive will to power over other men. This causes misfortune and evil. From this, he concluded that the will to survive and reproduce, as well as you yourself, are mistakes. Mr. Nietzsche is worse. He thought that the proper expression of your will was three-fold: the will to power, the will to overpower, and the will to war. He imagined a superman who wills to be superior over others and is a destroyer, not a builder. Mr. Nietzsche's will has inspired a few wars. Believe me, this is not what I had in mind. Both misguided thinkers took the simple little will to survive and reproduce that I gave you and extrapolated them into a vast, destructive, and sinister will to commit wrong. They are wrong. Also, someone should have told that crazy bastard Nietzsche that I am not dead—I just am not what he thought I was.

Your misinterpretation of the nature and importance of your will today causes you to judge it good or bad. I intended you to just do, but you now question what your will caused you to do. You question intent, or what your will made you do. In your concept of crime, for example, the severity of punishment depends on the intent of the criminal's will. If a killer's will is wanton and premeditated, then it is judged bad and you call it first-degree murder. If his intent was spontaneous and driven by passion, it is judged not as bad and you call it second-degree murder. If the killing is accidental and without willful intent, it is not very bad and you call it manslaughter. There is killing in nature but no such thing as murder. When one animal kills another, the event is not judged good or bad, it just is. Nature has no judges, no jails, and there is no evaluation of animals' will. In nature, the will is just the will and it simply does what is needed to survive.

Your will is everything and nothing works without it. It is your soul without the immortality.

The Nature of Religion

Humans, you are imaginative little shits. You take something small, simple, and understandable and blow it up into something big, complex, and confusing. You have so extended, mixed up, and confounded your feelings, intuition, and desire into what you call religion, even I have trouble untangling it. I have mixed feelings. On one hand your imagination entertains me. Nobody else could have conceived the fantastic ideas you have. But on the other, with these fantastic ideas, you often hurt yourselves, hurt others and disturbed my patterns. Let me explain the mess you made. The explanation is torturous because I must unravel in a few pages what it took you 2,000 years to bundle. We must wind our way through spirituality, feeling, happiness, meaning, belief, intuition, and truth before we can talk about religion.

I first have to separate spirituality and religion. They are not the same. Your spirituality is primitive, natural, and it exists in you. Primitive societies call it superstition and it occurs because primitive people fear the unknown. When people do not understand things they are usually afraid of harm. Because of this, spirituality is rooted in survival because it explains things which mitigates fear. Spirituality comes to you spontaneously and intuitively. Religion is different. Religion, which evolved from your spirituality, leads to strange practices, ideologies, and dogmas. It also causes you many problems when it evolves too far from the patterns. Of the two, religion is the most imaginative, elaborate, dangerous, entertaining, and furthest from my patterns.

One thing you are good at is talking about knowing what you do not understand. Spirituality is one of these things. You talk about how great it is but then disagree on what it is. Your religions' followers, psychics, cultists, spiritualists, seers, priests, and shamans not only have different definitions of spirituality but also incomplete ones. Each describes spirituality in unique ways and their descriptions are like describing your will or the color yellow: they describe its effects or consequences and not the thing itself. Curiously, none of you asks how you can understand something you disagree on and cannot coherently describe.

This is because you are complicated little bundles of feelings and thoughts that influence one another. Your feelings affect your thoughts and your thoughts affect your feelings. Significantly, what you feel becomes what you think and what you think becomes what you believe.

Therefore, your beliefs often are just extensions of your feelings. Your spirituality is one of these extensions. It is nothing more than your feelings and the beliefs derived from your feelings. It is a sentiment.

Your confusion comes from mixing up feelings and beliefs. You unknowingly slide back and forth between the two. When you describe your spirituality you are essentially describing your feelings. This explains why people describe their spirituality in different and special ways. Further, when you describe a feeling you do not describe it, rather you describe what the feeling feels like. And when you describe the ideas that come from your feelings, you describe the consequences of your feelings. This is why you have difficulty describing what spirituality essentially is. You can describe its effects satisfactorily, like your feelings, but you cannot describe what it is because you cannot describe what it is to feel, like the color yellow.

The relationship between feelings and beliefs becomes so tight you often cannot tell the difference. This explains why you often do not understand what you are talking about. You confuse yourself because they are different and you describe them as one. You think, for example, you are describing beliefs when you are really describing feelings. The point of all this is that your feelings, and the beliefs derived from them, are your spirituality. You spirituality is a sentiment, and it is all about feeling.

This is why most poets, artists, and other sensitive souls tend to be spiritual. They are inclined toward feeling instead of rationality. Your poets put feelings into words, painters put feelings on canvas, musicians put feelings in music, actors put feelings on stage, and sculptors put feelings in clay. The most sensitive among you are the most affected by feelings and the most likely to think in terms of their feelings. Spirituality comes naturally and intuitively to them.

But spirituality is more than just feeling. Rarely do you adopt attitudes and beliefs that make you feel bad. You never hear, for example, a spiritualist say, "My beliefs make me feel terrible," or "I can hardly stand my beliefs because they depress me." The most spiritual among you rarely get epiphanies from revelations or experiences that make them feel bad. Your epiphanies do not come from a poke in the eye with a sharp stick. Spirituality, therefore, is the attitudes and beliefs you adopt to make yourselves feel good. It is a way of seeing the world selectively so that you see only information that makes you feel better. It filters information, creating a presentation that makes you feel more secure, connected, and happy. This lets you see what you want to see. Your Mr. Freud called this mass delusion. Spirituality, therefore, is your delusional effort to enhance the feelings and beliefs that make you feel good.

Because each of you has different ideas about what makes you feel good, you naturally have different ideas about spirituality. How each of you accentuates pleasure and mitigates pain is highly personal and rather esoteric. You all do it differently, so you adopt different attitudes and beliefs that work for you. This explains why you have such difficulty explaining the nature of spirituality. When describing spirituality, each of you is essentially describing what beliefs make you feel good. Of course, this makes spirituality an inherently selfish thing, which fits with your inherently selfish natures, and comes from your instinct to survive. Pretty simple so far, but it is not the entire story.

As I mentioned, you are animals existing within natural patterns. One pattern is birth, life, reproduction, and death. Everything else is essentially pointless. This makes many of you very unhappy. So you imagine a unified and teleological world, a world that has meaning and purpose. You imagine the world you want and create in it, through addition and subtraction, the meaning you desire. An embracing world that caters to you, wants you, and makes you happy. For example, you predispose yourselves to love others, which makes you think they love you. This makes you feel good about humanity. To ease your fear of dying, you conceive of an afterlife. This way you persuade yourself that you have avoided the dreaded nothingness and will go somewhere to party after you die. You begin thinking everything is meaningfully connected, which makes you feel good because you are part of something. You no longer feel alone. You also discard attitudes and beliefs that cause angst, depression, and anxiety. What better way to create meaning and happiness in you lives than through spirituality?

But your beliefs change, especially when presented with better reasons for other beliefs. But changing spiritual beliefs that make you feel happy may make you feel unhappy. To avoid this you fortify your beliefs and make them faiths. You believe what you assume to be true and disregard all other beliefs. Your efforts to verify, intellectualize, quantify, or rationalize your spiritual beliefs invariably fail because you decide not to believe anything else.

Spirituality is based on your feelings, which makes it intensely personal and irrational. It cannot be verified; it must be taken on faith. Therefore, the attitudes and beliefs that comprise spirituality are not logical. They require the "leap of faith" that your Mr. Kierkegaard embraced. You must "leap" to them because your faith is intuitional, not rational. Many of your religious thinkers have stressed the importance of discounting rationality and adopting faith. Mr. Pascal, for example, said, "The heart has its reasons of which reason knows nothing," and your Mr. Augustine said, "Seek not to understand in order to believe, but [rather] believe in order to understand."

This also explains why doubt is spirituality's great enemy. If you have made the leap of faith you always know that your beliefs may be false. If you lose your faith you know that you risk losing the beliefs that make you happy. So, you remain blind and strident in your beliefs because you do not want to face the unhappy consequences of losing them. You will do most anything, as history has shown, to maintain them. Indeed, your Mr. Niebuhr, the American theologian, said, "Frantic orthodoxy is never rooted in faith but in doubt."

Your imagination gets so entertaining in these circumstances. You become like little kids earnestly defending the existence of Santa Claus. You commence solidifying and defending wrong assumptions that are based on your self-interests. You unilaterally assume beliefs that make you happy, harden them into a faith, and then defend them as true. You see this all the time. Many of your spiritualists believe that spirituality is truth. They claim that spirituality deals with a more real, transcendent and timeless world. This, of course, is the implication of Messrs. Kierkegaard, Pascal, and Augustine's statements. They imply that you can only understand the truth by adopting faith.

Your problem lies in the definition of the word truth. You are talking about two truths. One is a capital "T" truth that is a true, timeless, and universal philosophers' truth. The other is a small "t" kind of psychological, personal truth, a truth that is true to you individually. Only I know whether the capital "T" truth exists, but you have the ability to declare whether that personal small "t" truth exists. You can declare it because you believe it. Your spirituality therefore is not capital "T" truth but rather small "t" truth. It is your personal interpretation of what is true. This explains why different spiritual and religious groups each claim that their beliefs are uniquely true. The answer is they are— to them.

The point is that spirituality is not about truth but rather feeling. Truth has nothing to do with spirituality. The search for truth, as in your philosophy is actually a hindrance to your becoming spiritual.

I now can explain your religion. Religion is simply your institutionalized and ritualized spirituality. It is your spirituality hardened into ideologies, myths, and dogmas, each with different names. You call these ideologies things like Catholicism, Judaism, Confucianism, Hinduism, Islamism, and Presbyterianism. You call the myths things like God, heaven, hell, angels, and devils. And you call the dogmas things like good and evil, determinism and free will, and salvation and damnation. You imagine these things and then call them true. Because few of you agree what is true, you get mad with those who disagree with what you think is true and do things like go to war, sacrifice people, demonize unbelievers, impose artificial moralities and become generally intolerant.

You must appreciate the irony of this. Your simple instinct to survive, intuition, and clever mind collaborate to imagine incredible things. Your feeling of fear causes you to conceive of meaning, purpose, and happiness. You create elaborate ideological systems that serve this end, institutionalize them, and then argue over whose Rube Goldberg is the best. It all began rather benignly. Your early religions parroted natural morality. Your Ten Commandments, for example, preached the avoidance of things like killing, stealing, and adultery. But you got carried away and screwed everything up. You began imagining floods, Gardens of Eden, and heavens. Some religious thinkers imagined a place called Hell and your priests began threatening to send you there if you disagreed with them. Then your kings caught on to this proselytizing ruse and started using religion to support their states.

What irritates me the most is that you dragged me into this mess. Initially I was flattered to be the object of your attentions but you have used my name too many times for the wrong reasons. I am not a reason to go to war, I am not the cause of evil, and I am not all good. I am just a pattern in nature; I just am. By the way, I am irritated with your Pope for telling everyone he speaks for me. He does not and I do not appreciate his pretentiousness. Also, I do not like Mr. Dante's hell: it makes me look judgmental. I did get a good laugh out of Mr. Pascal when he said you should believe in me just in case I am true. Funny monks are so rare.

The Prioritization of Ideals

You are an argumentative, obstreperous, and contentious lot. You are always fighting and bickering. None of you seems to get along or agree on anything. Your nations fight, families feud, friends argue, neighbors quarrel, religions dispute and political parties brawl. The list is endless. Have you ever wondered why? Significant among the many reasons is your imagination. To enhance your survivability you conceive of various constructs, including ideas intended to help you live in peace. They began as simple rules of conduct derived from the morality that naturally evolved from your aggregating. These rules, you may recall, include such things as not killing or stealing. You call this justice. Some objected to being limited by these rules, a rule-less state that you call freedom. Finally, when a few objected to the selective application of these rules, you called the solution equality. These ideas served you so well that your imagination elevated them to what you call ideals, and you began describing them as timeless and universal imperatives. This was audacious. Your problems began when you started imaginatively misapplying these ideals for selfish reasons. The result has caused much of your contentiousness.

You have created many ideals, but your most important seem to be freedom, justice, and equality. I will discuss how these ideals affect you collectively later on, but now I will explain how they influence you individually. Although some of your thinkers like Mr. Plato would disagree, I assure you that none of these ideals exists in nature. They are meaningless within the patterns of nature. The other animals have nothing like your ideal of freedom, they have no concept of justice, and they definitely are not equal. Nobody, other than yourselves, created any special ideals for you.

It should come as no surprise then that these ideals often fail when you try to apply them within the patterns. You immediately come face to face with the stark difference between your imaginary ideals and my concrete reality. In fact, you become quite frustrated and angry when your ideals do not work the way you want. You usually blame each other, but mostly you blame me. Think of it: you create imaginary and unrealistic ideals, get angry when they fail, and then blame me! You have it backward: you are the problem, not me. I had nothing to do with creating your ideals, I do not make them fail, and I have better things to do than straighten out your mess. For me, this is like helping a child fix his broken toy.

Let me say that your ideals are not inherently wrong. They are quite clever. They do seem to help you navigate your constructs and enhance your survival. They seem to work best when you approximate them rather than take them literally. They appear to be most effective when you view them as normative concepts intended to guide yourselves. Whatever, they cause much of your contentiousness for three reasons.

First, none of you seems to agree on their definitions. Because you made them up, some of you have different ideas of what they mean. Some of you define freedom, justice, and equality differently. For example, some may define justice as individual justice and others as social justice. Both definitions are problematic because they are contradictory. Some of you extend the meaning of justice for the individual to include the collective group. In doing so, your notion of what justice means is lost because you combined two words. This combined meaning then is not the same as the meanings of the individual words. This explains why a consequence of your social justice is often injustice. Second, your ideals commonly conflict. Freedom often limits justice and equality, justice often limits freedom and equality, and equality invariably limits freedom and causes injustice.

Finally, because you disagree about their meanings—and they indeed conflict, each of you is free to apply them selectively and selfishly. And many of you do. For example, a minority might view what you call race quotas as equality while the majority might view them as loss of freedom. Or your poor might view redistribution of wealth policies as justice and equality, while the rich might see injustice, the loss of freedom, and inequality. Most of you use your ideals for ends that serve personal interests.

So how can we put the wheel back on your broken toy? How can you mitigate your disagreements, contentiousness, and fighting? The answer is right in front of you. Define your ideals, agree on their definitions, and then prioritize them. Your *Random House Dictionary* is not bad but my dictionary, *The Divine Dictionary*, is better. Let me use it to define your three principal ideals. Freedom means personal and political independence, immunity from controls and duties, and generally to be unrestricted. It particularly means freedom from control of other people. Justice means to be fair, honest, and equitable. And equality means to have the same rights or privileges. These are the divine definitions, and I admonish you to agree on them.

Now your challenge is to apply these ideals timelessly and universally. You must apply them to everyone uniformly, and the same through time, or they will not work. Ultimately, if there are exceptions, they will lose all ability to compel because individuals will apply them only when they want. They will lose their force because too many people will not feel obligated to follow them.

I do not like being the bearer of bad news, but I think you will never make these ideals of yours work timelessly and universally together. The reason is simple: they constitutionally conflict. Therefore, you must prioritize them. You must agree among yourselves on their relative importance. If you could, you would all apply them uniformly and therefore agree on the relative importance of your beliefs. You would no longer be able to apply them selfishly. Your ideals then would be the same for all under the same circumstances. The benefits would be stupendous. You would have fewer conflicts, and your species would become less contentiousness.

It really is none of my business how you rank these ideals. You should be aware, however, that none means anything without freedom. All of your other ideals presuppose freedom. Justice is important, but for what if you are not free? Some of you might say that if there were perfect justice, freedom would be unnecessary. I disagree because one must be free in order to be just. Indeed, the lack of your freedom is injustice itself. Equality is the least valuable of your ideals. One of you even called it idealized envy. You cannot be equal without freedom because you must have the freedom to be equal. Further, the ideal of equality is based on your ideal of justice. You even say to be equal is justice; therefore you must have justice to be equal. When you define equality as equal opportunity and equal treatment under your laws, you appeal to justice as the justification. The point of all this is that if you have to err, do so on the side of freedom. With freedom, the other ideals are attainable. Without it, they are meaningless.

One last oblique comment: do not confuse ideals with values. They are different. You create the ideals of freedom, justice, and equality, but love comes to you instinctually. When you created meaning, you discovered much of it comes from other people. As a result some of you value love more than justice. However, most of you increasingly value things over people. If you ever decide to prioritize your values like your ideals, I suggest you consult your Mr. Tolstoy. It is a long story but his character Mr. Ilych showed the way by dying. When you are looking into the abyss of nothingness, what is valuable becomes conspicuous. I think most of you will find that things like property and prestige mean little, and relationships, family, and love mean a lot. Some of you are fortunate and learn Mr. Tolstoy's lesson in life and some of you do not.

The Nature of Wealth

I find the topic of wealth rather prosaic, but we need discuss it because you spend so much time pursuing it. Wealth is essentially security, and in particular the security to survive. However, you have made if far more than this. Your imagination has blown it way out of proportion and your desire for it has caused many of you to accumulate unnecessarily. Too many pursue wealth only for wealth's sake. To complicate matters, much of what you do and think seems to collide here. Wealth is the nexus where many of your desires, emotions, and ideals come together and unravel.

You value wealth and ownership of property. These are your concepts; they mean nothing to me. Your imagination has created these concepts and confused you. Ultimately, property has no value in and of itself within the patterns. Only you give things value. You have also come to think of property and value as things and, increasingly as money. Most now think that money is the same as property because they are fungible. Many of you have come to value money for itself.

Add to this brew your concept of ownership, and you have a recipe for mischief. The concept of ownership also does not exist in nature. You conceived of this long ago when your Mr. Jesus said, "Render therefore unto Caesar things that are Caesar's and unto God the things that are God's." Why he brought me into the picture I do not know. Things were not mine originally, they just were. Not only did he misconstrue what was mine but also presumptuously gave you ownership of what was not mine. This premise has caused you most of your problems with wealth.

Once this audacious assumption was made, it was only logical that you would proceed to argue over who owns what and how much. You have engaged in endless propaganda, battles and wars over this subject. On one side are your Messrs. Locke, Montesquieu, Hume, Madison, Hamilton, and Jefferson, who all said liberty is the unequal right to property. They said the purpose of your governments is to protect the different and unequal faculties of acquiring property. On the other side are your Messrs. Plato, Seneca, More, Fourier, Blanc, Marx, Engles, and Lenin, who said, "From each his ability, to each his need." I do not want to get into this squabble. Let me just say that in nature there is no ownership and nobody gets anything according to their need.

Your invention of money was most ingenuous and useful. Money is just your pecuniary system of equivalents and a way to keep score. You agree among yourselves that a certain amount of money is the same as some thing, when in reality you know that it is not. Money itself is worthless. It is a concept, a piece of metal, a scrap of paper, or the number of an account. It has no value and your system works only as long as all of you agree that it does. If you disagree, which is often, your artificial economies based on money fail and other things become valuable, like gold, sustenance, and ammunition. Your ancient Mr. Plato banned money from his utopian Republic and your Mr. Aristotle eschewed money because all it did was beget more money and not necessities. What I find so interesting is that you spend your short and purposeless existences valuing that which has no value. You are forever accumulating banknotes that must be left with new owners when you die. You have draped the world in money and lost sight of the natural sources of your existence. As your Mr. Marx said, you have become dominated by an alien entity of dead matter that has no master. That entity is money.

Your concept of money causes you trouble for many reasons. One is your own desire. Your Mr. Buchan once said that your world is a battlefield of limitless, unsatisfied wishes and desires which money makes conspicuous. It makes concrete the sensation of wanting as a clock does the sensation of passing time. Money is frozen desire. It is your happiness in abstract. It opens up worlds of pleasure to those who possess it and delivers countless miseries to those who do not. It makes concrete your desires and wishes. Money becomes desirable when it incorporates your wishes because it is the medium and arbiter of your needs and wants. Money also represents freedom to you, a coined liberty. It is the Magna Carta of your freedom because with it you are free to do what you want. Ultimately, your intense competition for money derives from your unlimited desires and yearning for freedom.

Your concepts of wealth, ownership, and money cause you so many problems that I do not have the time or inclination to discuss them all. Let me just say that money displaces many of your other values, tends to destroy your ethics and puts you permanently at war with each other and nature. When your concept of money enters your system of values, it tends to displace your other values, like love and friendship, as well as your ideals like justice and equality. My point is that money does not offer you love, friendship, justice, or equality; it only offers convenience and a little false security. I think your Mr. Lincoln said that money itself is not important, but its absence can be mighty inconvenient.

The ultimate irony of your accumulation of wealth is that it erodes your artificial constructs, which in turn diminishes your wealth. You created your constructs for security, which wealth embodies, and then wealth depletes your constructs. When your constructs fail, you lose wealth and security. This is because your wealth detaches you from the patterns of nature. The more abundance you acquire, the more you imagine yourselves above these patterns, the more your imagination is released, and the more you start believing things that defy nature. You come to believe sustenance and shelter are easily had, you commence devaluing what the most ambitious and talented among you have to offer, you take for granted that which you have wrested from nature, your moral codes gradually corrupt and you naturally sink into depravity and decadence. You see this process repeated throughout your history: societies begin with vigor, grow, become rich, decay, and eventually fail.

The Nature of Sexuality

As I mentioned in my opening remarks you have two basic instincts and sexuality is one of them. You do not need any lecture from me regarding its nature; you know it instinctively. I only bring it up is because it influences so much of your lives. I am going to explain how your imagination, ideas, and constructs have utterly confounded this instinct.

Let me start by describing the sex life of the Rhesus monkey. Of all the animals, the Rhesus is among your closest kin. If you had your way your sex life would be the same as that of this monkey. Rhesus monkeys live in loose bands of males and females. The females experience estrus, or periods when they are fertile and receptive sexually. When they come into estrus they copulate with all of the males in the tribe- like an orgy. At least one or two females are always in estrus and engaging in coitus. The males are naturally attracted to the youngest female monkeys because they are the most fecund. After copulation, the males wander off and the females raise the young because only they can produce and nourish offspring. Nobody, including fathers, mothers, and offspring know who the true fathers are.

The beauty of this natural pattern of sexuality accrues to both sexes. When the females are in estrus they get all the sex they want and when they are not the males leave them alone. They are left free to raise their young which satisfies their nurturing instincts. Because there are always a few females in estrus the males cannot wait to get up in the morning to see who is available for sex. The males get all the sex they want with a variety of females. When the males finish they are free to pursue their wanderlust without obligations. It is a simple natural pattern of nature that has been going on for thousands of years, it produces prodigious numbers of young Rhesus monkeys to perpetuate their species and makes for very happy monkeys.

Then you came along. Observe what would happen if you applied your sexual mores to the Rhesus monkey. First, you would dispense with the loose bands of males and females and require everyone to pair up, marry, and practice monogamy. One male with one female for life tied by a solemn oath to love, honor, and obey. There would be no more orgies. Because one female is now responsible for satisfying one male's sexual desire she is expected to be always available, estrus or not. The males now are frustrated because only one female cannot satisfy them so they are forever in want. The males and females are no longer free to wander off but rather bound to live together. The predictable results are frustrated males who must cope with complaining females and captive females who must deal with controlling males. In such an unnatural state they increasingly fight, criticize, complain and blame the other for their loss of freedom. Promiscuity and adultery are severely punished through societal disapprobation or legal sanctions. Any female who strays is punished and any sexually frustrated male who masturbates is shamed. Any gender that harasses or stalks the other is fined. Males incapable of controlling their sexual instincts are jailed if they engage in prostitution or rape or have sex with juvenile females. If their solemn pact of marriage fails, they face divorce courts, divorce attorneys and laws covering such things as custody of offspring, visitation rights and property distribution. Either may have continuing obligations such as child support and alimony. If they fail to meet these obligations they will be fined, have judgments issued against them, have their wages garnished or be denied work. Some may even lose their freedom. And you wonder why in this scenario the male and female Rhesus monkeys, like yourselves become so discontent, sexually frustrated and unhappy.

But it is much worse than this. Your artificial ideas and constructs create a panoply of intractable problems for your societies unknown to the monkeys. Your marriage requirement introduces lines of descent that bring numerous problems involving wealth and inheritance. Emotions such as possessiveness, envy, and jealousy become rampant due to the exclusiveness of your marriage and sexual constructs. These cause complicating emotions such as anger, resentment, and rejection when one spouse cheats. Those capable of maintaining this unrealistic pact are usually rewarded with marriage counselors and domestic violence.

With marriage you create legitimate and illegitimate children—and the latter spend their lives stigmatized. With divorce you create children with a host of problems including abandonment, loss of identity and difficulty in relationships. And if this is not bad enough your societies are forever compelled to suppress sexually deviant behaviors that are not problems for the Rhesus monkey. These include pornography, bigamy, prostitution, polygamy, homosexuality, bestiality, voyeurism and incest. The list of sexual deviations is virtually endless. Your sexual lives are now a mass of confusion and frustration. But your problems have only begun.

Your cleverness also is increasingly causing confusion of gender roles and functions. Because you think you are above my patterns you have come to feel free to create your own gender roles. Each of you thinks you are individually more important than the natural role you play and, too often, more important than the role someone else plays. One of the consequences is your war of roses, which is just a power struggle. You carry on this interminable, internecine war between the sexes that has no point or resolution. I am appalled at your most recent manifestation of this struggle, which is feminism. Some of your females now want equality. They want to do everything the male does. It is so bad that that in some more "advanced" civilizations the natural roles of males and females are actually reversed. The female provides and the male nurtures. Your cleverness has put your genders at odds with their essential human natures. I have news for both genders: you are not equal, equality is an imaginary ideal, each of you have different strengths and weaknesses, your artificial equality is only as good as your artificial constructs that enforce it and none of you will ever be happy trying to be what you are not.

I made you different for good reasons. I designed each gender for certain purposes which succored your survivability and ability to reproduce. The males are the protectors and providers. To accomplish this I made them bigger, stronger, and more aggressive. The females are the bearers and nurturers. This is why I gave them a uterus, breasts, and big hips. This is just the way it is. You can create new ideas, imagine different worlds, and build new constructs all you want, but nothing will change this unalterable pattern. What bothers me the most is that you seem to have forgotten that it is a cooperative effort and not competitive. Each gender has a special purpose within the patterns of nature and both are necessary for your continued existence.

III

GOD'S REMARKS ON THE NATURE OF HUMANS COLLECTIVELY

To make matters worse, you are not satisfied with just screwing up yourselves individually but seem intent on screwing up everyone else as well. You just do not like the way I organized you collectively so you endeavor to rearrange your associations to your liking. You are driven to arrange yourselves in increasingly complex and artificial ways to make your collective associations conform to what you imagine. Your imagination creates artificial collective structures like society, law, morality, and religion, which you then impress, like a waffle iron, onto your human natures. The results are very strange indeed. You get things like wars, injustice, inequality, anarchy, criminality, and immorality. These new structures increase your confusion, further detach you from the way things are, and make your lives miserable.

Freedom, Justice, and Equality

In the last section I addressed you individually. I mentioned that as individuals you conceive of your ideals of freedom, justice, and equality. I endeavored to disabuse you of the belief that these ideals are timeless and universal by explaining that they do not exist in nature. You created them for your safety and survival. Now I need to return to this topic and describe you collectively.

These concepts take on special significance when you aggregate because you use them as basis for your constructs. They are literally the foundation for many of your constructs like civilization, society, government, law, politics, and morality. You are forever using them as justifications, but do not completely understand them. You revere these concepts but they confuse you. Your use of them is like experiencing some event in your childhood that silently influences your beliefs and actions. You forgot the event long ago, you are not truly aware of what happened, you never evaluated whether your reaction to the event was warranted, you do not know if the event was true, you never even investigated it, and yet the event continues to superintend your life. You continue to assume blindly that the event was true and act accordingly. Like the forgotten event, these ideals unknowingly influence your actions.

These concepts are literally figments of your imagination, which is why you have such difficulty squaring them with reality. The obvious consequence is that when you use these ideals to create your constructs, your constructs are never perfect. They always have some deficiency that must be corrected. This causes much of your frustration with yourselves and your constructs. You are incapable of achieving that which you imagine.

Some of your more freewheeling thinkers claim that these ideals do exist in nature and point to your rationality and mathematics as proof. They claim that you can divine certain truths from nature, like mathematics, with your reason. They claim that mathematics is perfect. I am sorry to disappoint you but this simply is not true. You are a limited creature and you can only know so much. Your mathematics is just the highest manifestation of your rationality and your rationality is limited because it is only as good as your premises. It is a house of cards because your premises, conceived by your imagination are often wrong. For example, you assume that you are entitled to freedom, justice, equality, and then reason from there, but there is no freedom, justice, or equality in nature. It is like planning to raise a herd of unicorns. You obtain financing, buy a ranch, and arrange for feed but then cannot populate your ranch because unicorns do not exist. All this makes you an audacious little twit.

Freedom is your most cherished ideal. You always aspire to it. What you seek are actually two freedoms, freedom from nature and freedom from each other. As I have said, the first freedom does not exist because nature ineluctably limits you. The seasons, scarcity, and other animals conspire to limit your freedom in nature. Your idea of freedom simply does not exist in nature. The second, the one you usually think of, is freedom from control of others. This freedom, however, is just an average between anarchy and totalitarianism. At one extreme, the unfettered state of anarchy may bring the loss of safety. The other extreme, totalitarianism, sometimes brings safety but more often danger. In either case you are not free. The consequence is that you are forever attempting to juggle the mathematical equation of nature to achieve a maximum state of freedom. The best result you can achieve is a balanced freedom somewhere in the middle. Your Mr. Mill best described this state of affairs. He asked not what freedom is but what are its legitimate limits? He pointed out that the main one is obviously a limit on your violent and aggressive natures to achieve safety. How much to limit your behaviors to achieve freedom is one of your most confounding questions. It has been debated by some of your greatest thinkers.

Like freedom, there is no justice in the patterns of nature. You claim that you are entitled to just treatment. You claim, or assume, that this is one of your rights. Originally, you created the concept of justice to enforce your social contracts for safety. In this respect your justice is a limiting process intended to control your natural instincts. It mediated and equalized your imaginary rights. In nature, for example, stronger beasts subdue weaker beasts. It could be said that this is the stronger beasts' natural right. But the weaker of your kind do not like this, so you subtract from the strongers' right and add to the weakers'. You call this social justice. Consequently, your justice has become just another name for power, the power to give and take rights to bring about equalization. This judicial leap of imagination began with your Mr. Aristotle and his idea of distributive justice. Your Mr. Bentham expanded it in his theory of utilitarianism or happiness for most. I will not go into detail on these interpretations of justice because I have already discussed the topic. Let me just say that you will never achieve your concept of justice by committing injustice.

Equality is your worst ideal. You use the word loosely. It derives from your justice. I distinguish two kinds of equality, one real and the other artificial. Real equality is just that, perfectly equal. Of course, as you know, this does not exist in nature. You are, in truth, perfectly unequal. Some of you are just stronger, smarter or more handsome than others. You created artificial equality to even the scales, prevent oppression, and enhance your safety and economic security. These things increased the survivability of some. But this desire to be equal is really masked envy, or the desire to have others' superior ability to survive. Your Mr. Oliver Wendell Holmes said the demand for equality "is [just] idealized envy." To achieve this unnatural equality and satiate your envy, some of you have developed legal and political constructs that endeavor to bring it about. Many of you confuse these real and artificial forms of equality, a state of affairs I believe you call denial.

One recent manifestation of these imaginary ideals is what you call your rights. You assume that freedom, justice, and equality exist, and that you have some right to them which you then use to justify more rights. Your Mr. Jefferson, for example, held that you have the self-evident and inalienable rights of life, liberty, and the pursuit of happiness, which he presumptuously thought I gave you. I have news for you: there are no rights in nature. I did not inculcate freedom, justice, or equality in nature. You are not free or equal. There is no justice in the world and you have no rights. These imaginary rights of yours are really just tradeoffs. To give a right to one individual requires taking a right from another. To some, for example, granting the right of freedom from want means violating the right of others to keep the fruits of their efforts. Also, the right not to be discriminated against means another's right to associate with whom they choose must be attenuated. The list of tradeoffs over rights is endless. The only rights you have in nature, if you could call them such, are the rights to try to survive and reproduce. You could be better described as right-less in nature.

Because these rights are sentiments you apply them selectively and subjectively. For example, you have added to the list disabled rights, gender rights, age rights, racial rights, sexual rights and so on. Obviously, none of them exists in nature. Your incessant demand for rights poses a dilemma because if you extend them too far no one would have rights. You would end up in anarchy because, as I have explained, your rights conflict: when you confer one right, you take away another. If everyone had rights then nobody would have rights. What you are doing is confusing rights with privileges.

This raises interesting and predictable consequences that you may not have considered. First, your ideals, along with their attendant rights, have created layers of contradictions. You demand freedom but take freedom, you demand justice but perpetrate injustice, you demand equality but cause inequality, and you eschew discrimination but discriminate. Second, your freedom, justice, and equality come only by force. To bring about these ideals, you must employ the very thing you intended them to prevent. For example, you created the concept of freedom to be free from coercive forces but have discovered that you must employ coercive force to achieve it. The truth is that only through coercion can you achieve any semblance of these ideals. Your Mr. Jefferson conspicuously made this point when he said, "…that to secure these rights, Governments are instituted among men…" You must use the coercive force of your construct of government to achieve these imaginary ideals and ostensible rights. Your concept of social justice, which is a synonym for power is the justification you use to implement these ideals.

I want you to consider your utter arrogance and presumptuousness in this matter. You claim that freedom, justice, and equality are self-evident, that I granted them, and that you are entitled to them. You have a word for this, hubris. You arrogantly assume you are me and then proceed to grant yourselves these privileges. I have news for you—I never created them, the other animals do not have them, and you are not special.

The Nature of Civilization

It has been so interesting to watch you organize yourself collectively. You started as individuals but immediately began developing these highly imaginative, often useful, and sometimes awful forms of social organization. You seem to have this innate inclination to civilize yourselves. You seem to prefer this to anarchy. Anarchy is your word, not mine. The other animals have no such thing as anarchy because for them everything fits. However, you do not like how I arranged things in nature, so you conceived of civilization and called what I had created anarchy. It was only after you imagined the word civilization that its opposite, anarchy, appeared. Just think how untoward and outrageous your claim is that I created chaos and you created order. I am offended.

Civilization is your advanced state of social development. It is a gradation. The higher the social development of your societies the more you consider them civilized. Higher civilization, for example, represents to you a more advanced social organization over previous less organized societal developments that you often call savage and barbaric. Your primitive societies' were maintained by kinship bonds which you consider primitive. Your more advanced, civilized societies are held together primarily by your imaginary constructs and ideas which are really myths. The constructs include such things as economic, governmental, and legal systems and the ideas or myths of freedom, justice, and equality. Your early civilizations were the natural systems that arose when you aggregated but your imagination has made them more elaborate.

The principal reason you civilize is your desire for safety, security and convenience. Many of your early civilizations did this, which improved many lives. Many of your problems began when you started thinking you could use your imaginary idea of civilization to ameliorate yourselves. You have come to equate civilization with amelioration. But civilization per se is not ameliorative; it is just a higher degree of social organization. Your constructs in civilization do not necessarily represent improvement. For example, many of your highly evolved social organizations are brutal, and their citizens would be better off in my state of nature.

Your idea of amelioration is curious. Some amelioration occurs in nature. Animals adapt physically and instinctually to changing environments which is an ameliorative process. But nature has nothing like your wholesale societal change, social engineering and organization for the betterment of your species. You have been most imaginative with this concept which makes it a very complicated topic. It is as if you continually fiddle with part of a big mathematical equation to improve the outcome. The problem is that in nature's equation all the components are necessarily connected; everything is cause and effect. The equation is perfect and when you change one part another is altered. One part may improve but another gets worse. Some of the components you use to alter the equation include your institutions, your societal paradigms and your personal beliefs.

I give you credit, though, because many of your institutions are improving. Your democracies, for example, are an improvement over monarchies. However, they brought the tyranny of the majority, a situation very similar to being subject to the will of a monarch. It also seems evident that many of your societal paradigms are improving. Your societies experience changing paradigms, or paradigm shifts. A good one is your new belief in trial by jury rather than confession by torture. However, your jury system has its problems. The most intelligent and educated among you no longer make up juries. I also think many of your personal beliefs are improving. Most of you, for example, once believed in fate; you believed that you could do little to change your circumstances. When you discarded this belief in favor of free will and began laboring for better circumstances your lives truly did get better. Perhaps the best consequence of this change is your science which has dramatically improved your circumstances. However, science has also brought you incredible weapons that could eradicate your species. Your amelioration in these issues, like the mathematical equation has been a matter of tradeoffs.

One essential part of nature's equation, however, that continually thwarts your ameliorative efforts is your human nature. You can improve your institutions, societal paradigms and personal beliefs all you want but they will do little without some improvement in your natures. You think you are the measure of all these things and you envision civilization, implement it and superintend it. But your civilization is only as good as you are. And therein lays your problem: you are not inherently good, you are selfish and your human nature is not improving. In fact, your nature has remained the same since creation. Your Mr. Euripides, who wrote *Medea* over 2,400 years ago, describes the same human emotions of love, hate, jealousy, and fear that exist in you today. What keeps you from achieving the answers you desire is this fixed and unalterable part of nature's equation. It counterbalances your efforts to improve and confounds your efforts at amelioration.

I have heard many of your thinkers challenge this truth. They claim that a person can be educated to change their nature through beliefs but I must tell you that this is impossible. Some of you are stupid, some lazy and some just do not want to learn. Furthermore, even if you wanted to you simply do not have the resources to educate every man, woman, and child to change their beliefs and ultimately their natures. Your puny will can do only so much to alter the patterns of nature.

As you know, your advanced social organizations have innumerable problems. For example, they often do not bring safety or security. Sometimes they even make your lives less safe and secure. Why? It is because your idea of what constitutes civilization is one of your imagination's most amorphous and meaningless concepts. Consequently, like most of your imaginary ideas many of you interpret what constitutes a civilization differently and for selfish reasons. Different societies develop different ideas of what constitutes a better civilization and subsequently evolve different forms of civilizations or cultures. Your Muslims believe Islam and Islamic law are the most civilized, your Swedish think their socialism is more civilized and your Americans think their constitutional democracy is more civilized. But these different higher forms of social organization that you sometimes call states often quarrel and you end up being the fodder when their words come to blows. The result is you get less safety and more insecurity because you cannot agree among yourselves what constitutes higher civilization.

Using your imaginary concepts of justice and equality compounds your problems with civilization. You use these concepts and then proceed to violate them. When you endeavor to achieve these ostensibly ameliorative ideals through your social engineering the other end of the equation changes and you end up with the same injustice and inequality. In your constitutional democracy, for example, you proclaim freedom then take freedom through tyranny of the majority. You proclaim justice then commit injustice when you create a progressive tax system based on "from each his ability to each his need." And you proclaim equality then confer certain rights on some causing inequality because others' rights are violated. The truth is that your civilization is a fragile pane of glass that is easily cracked, chipped, broken and shattered.

It should not surprise you by now that many of your problems stem from this collision of your civilization and human natures. Some of your ideas and constructs are getting better but not you. You are an animal and many of the contradictions you experience arise because you layered civilization's rules over your human nature. It is like making one of your waffles from batter—the process of making the waffle-form causes a mess. Your batter natures are not easily manipulated or acculturated. Your natures naturally resist your civilization's endless rules of conduct. It is like imagining a panoply of artificial and imaginary rules and then endeavoring to impose them on a pack of wild dogs. You are trying to engineer these wild dogs individually and collectively to make them something they are not. The collision between your instincts and your civilizations' imperatives causes inevitable and predictable behaviors which you find pejorative. In the cosmic scheme of things these really are not bad behaviors but natural in nature. They are only bad because they do not conform to your concept of civilization. Because you cannot change your human natures you continually try to control, modify, superintend, suppress and direct them. This explains many of the behavioral maladies in your societies today as well as your prisons.

When you filtered your instincts for survival and reproduction through the rules and regulations of civilization you began labeling many of your emotions as bad. What was once a good, or at least neutral, emotion suddenly became awful in your mind. Survival became selfishness, desire to survive became pride (you naturally believe you are worthy of surviving), taking to survive became theft, wanting what another had to survive became envy, reproduction became lust, resting became indolence, fighting for existence became anger, vigilance against your enemies became hate, fleeing when confronted with danger became fear, eating too much became gluttony (in nature you often feasted when there was a surfeit in order to survive drought), just wanting to preserve what is yours became jealousy and saving your kill for the future became greed. All these words are your descriptions of what happens when the rules of your civilization collide with your natural human nature.

You have created a virtual world built on contradictions.

I find it so amusing when wonder why your world is so full of irony and contradiction. You imagine imaginary things, creating contradictions and then wonder why contradictions exist. Nature has no contradictions because everything fits. You make the contradictions. You want to be altruistic but are selfish, you want humility but are prideful, you want people to be satisfied but they are envious and jealous, you want love but you hate, you want to control sexuality but get frustration and lust, you want to be productive but are indolent, you want peace but get anger and vengeance, you want safety but cannot eradicate fear and you want people to share but only get gluttony and greed. And then you blame everything but your own human natures for these disturbing contradictions. You blame the devil, your lack of willpower or your childhood. Above all you blame me. The real irony is that these emotions are natural while your belief that contradictions exist is the illusion.

The Relationship between the Individual and Society

Your imagination has set up an artificial contest between your individuality and your societies. Earlier I mentioned that you are individuals first. You are an independent animal just like all the rest. Put a dog in a pack or a monkey in a tribe and they are still an individual dog and monkey. Hermits are no less human than the rest of you. When all is said and done you are born alone, live alone and die alone. You are yourself and not what others make of you. Your civilizing constructs, on the other hand, are collective processes that diminish your individuality in order to make you compatible with your communities and societies. What you have done is elevate this contentious process to a war that now pervades much of your existence and causes many of your problems.

Your constructs of states, societies, and civilizations are collective entities. They define you in terms of the group, not as individuals. Consequently, your societal constructs have pitted your individuality against your collective groups. Groups must restrict individuality to exist. They are built on the renunciation of your individual instincts. As I mentioned in my introductory remarks you are naturally an aggressive animal. I made you this way to enhance your survival. But this aggressive instinct confounds your collective constructs. They must control your aggressive instinct to thrive. In fact, the greatest threat to your societal constructs is your aggressive nature. Perpetuating your collective constructs are parents and institutions. They have the unenviable task of civilizing each new generation of heathen children.

One reason you are a bundle of contradictions is because your civilization and its rules are superimposed over your human natures. This naturally creates contradictions because the two are incompatible. Dogs are not bundles of contradictions. This forcing process manifests in the inevitable conflict between individuals and societies, a contest ultimately waged in your own minds. Your mind tugs you one way and your nature tugs another. Your mind forever imagines new things that your bodily instincts resist. You must appreciate the irony of this. You created your civilizing constructs to free yourselves from nature and each other but all you did was replace them with your constructs. Now many of you desire freedom from your own constructs or, to put it more precisely, freedom from your own imaginations.

The essence of this contest is between collectivism and individuality and it pervades your existence. You see it in your governments, societies, laws, civilizations, moralities, customs, traditions, religions and attitudes. Your increasing collectivization, like your economic system of socialism, makes you like ants in an ant colony. You become increasingly unimportant as individuals and your support of the collective group increasingly measures your value. Like ants your purpose in life is to support the colony. You are born into the colony, expected to spend your lives working for the colony and then die. You have no existence beyond this. You are unimportant as an individual being. This highly artificial process detaches you from my patterns of nature.

Some of the most significant contradictions of this collectivization process are in your desire for freedom and security which necessarily require you to be responsible. On one hand you desire freedom but on the other you desire security. However, to achieve security each of you must voluntarily limit your freedom. It is a tradeoff between freedom and security. However, you must have responsibility to willingly limit your freedoms. But you resist responsibility (and its counterpart accountability) because it also limits your freedom. The other animals do not face these equational oxymorons because, unlike you, they do not have constructs that endeavor to guarantee security through personal responsibility.

Your societal constructs control your behaviors in a number of ways. Some of these superintending forces include culture, guilt and ethics. Your cultures create smothering customs and traditions intended to make you conform. Your Mr. Freud explained that your societies only can exist if they create a conscience and imbed a sense of guilt to suppress your aggressive instincts. The other animals do not have guilt. A jackal does not experience guilt or contrition when it steals another's kill. With you the group uses conscience and guilt to force compliance and prevent you from acting differently as individuals. More advanced societies use ethics to control your behavior. Ethics create rules and obligations that restrict your individuality and enforce compliance.

Many problems confounding you are simply manifestations of these contradictions. Collectivization makes you unhappy because it restricts your aggressive instincts. Most of you chafe at societies' restrictions. In your most advanced societies you exchange happiness for security. This may sound like a bargain but the price is very steep. Guilt caused by your conscience causes a permanent internal unhappiness. These suppressors cause most mental abnormalities such as malaise, depression and dissatisfaction. In fact, you have become neurotic because you have so severely suppressed your natures. Your civilizations literally depend on you being neurotic. Civilization is essentially a neurotic process. I do not have much more to say on this topic except to express my amazement at how much suppression of you instincts you tolerate. Where you end up will be interesting to see.

You have set up an eternal tug of war between the individual and the collective group and the individuals appear to be losing. Your collectivistic constructs have become increasingly involuntary, coercive and draconian. Everywhere they conspire against your individuality, dictating your obligations and demanding the surrender of your individual freedom. But you yearn for individual freedom and will always resist. To understand this read your past thinkers. Your Mr. Rousseau championed you in nature; your Mr. Jefferson claimed for you individually inalienable rights to life, liberty and the pursuit of happiness, and your Mr. Emerson said you should be self-reliant and independent from any group that thinks it knows your obligations better than you. These thinkers man the front lines in your ongoing war with the group.

Your imagination has created the constructs that you desire freedom from and the consequences you wish to escape. Your artificial constructs have set you up for an eternal struggle between your individuality and your collective societal entities. You truly are your own worst enemy.

The Nature of Society

I now have discussed your construct of civilization and its relationship to you individually. Let us now explore the nature of your collective groups within civilization which are your societies. Your highly developed societal organizations just blow my mind. These teratoid entities are so strange and detached from what I intended that making sense of them is hard. They defy common sense. Your cleverness has worked overtime on this one.

The battlegrounds for you ongoing war between your individuality and collectivizing civilizations are your societies. It began rather benignly. To enhance your survivability, security, and reproducibility you voluntarily organized into small familial bands and clans. These small, simple arrangements worked well. Any societal stratification was based mostly on might. These organizations thrived and you multiplied. You created simple economic systems such as markets that satisfied your material needs. Collaterally, you developed customs that supported the organizations and you called them morally good. Everything was going well until your imagination took over and your organizations started getting away from you.

Then these entities began evolving further and further from your control. Many of you began treating these separate and imaginary entities as if they were real. Your imagination invested imaginary needs in these increasingly complex social structures, needs that exceeded what you require for survival and reproduction. You developed complex laws, massive institutions, powerful political parties, propagandized educational systems and draconian religious dogmas. These developments reinforced and perpetuated your imaginary and unrealistic societies.

You gave them unprecedented power over yourselves. Gradually and imperceptibly these entities coerced you individually to conform and comply. They began convincing you that in nature you are essentially collective and not individuals. They started devaluing individuality because if you are free individuals they could not thrive. Now your collective societies are so dominant they are the norm and you the individual are the exception. So, you are now a pawn in your own socialization process. You have lost control of your unrealistic social creations.

Your societies are like a unicorn; they only exist in your minds. They are just imaginary obligations, rules, duties and relationships. As evidence observe when your civilizations fail how your societies disappear like a puff of smoke in a strong breeze. Some of you so vehemently want these imaginary societies to be real they invest tremendous power into these collective nothings. They attach great importance to these societies because they do not like my patterns in nature. They want to use your construct of society to change my patterns through social engineering. To achieve this they insist that societies dictate duties, ascribe obligations and choose for you. The predictable result is that your societies are increasingly at war with your naturally individualistic human nature.

The qualities ascribed to these societies—such as the phrases social weal, social justice, social security and social safety net—are meaningless phrases. To whom do they apply? Not to the individual but some imaginary collective social entity. These concepts exist only because you conceived of the construct society. Put another way, if you had never imagined society then there would be no need for these qualities. These are non-existent concepts you created for a non-existent entity you call society. An equation of nothing plus nothing equals nothing. These phrases become blank palates and free-floating ideas which you interpret differently. Some think social weal means big government is to provide for some while others think it means to be left alone. These terms are really intended to provide security and survivability for some at the expense of others.

Then it gets interesting, or perhaps tragic, because you start fighting over whose definition of society is the best. Think of what you do: you create a non-existent entity, society, ascribe to it non-existent characteristics, such as social weal, and then fight over whose definition is correct. If you cannot agree on these societies' characteristics how can you possibly agree on which is best? I have news for you: nature has nothing like your highly evolved and complex social organizations. They are foreign to my patterns, the other animals do not have them and you are an individual. They are products of your imagination and you are fighting over unicorns.

The interesting question is why you allow yourselves to become entangled in these artificial social webs. Why do you so willingly give up your individual freedoms? Why do your simple familial social organizations grow into such hulking monstrosities? Your Mr. Emerson explained the dynamics of this phenomenon and, in the process, uncovered the true nature of your societal constructs. The answer is found within the nature of the group. Only conformity and compliance can maintain your groups. Individuality is the antithesis to the group because if you are individuals the group could never form. Conformity becomes the highest virtue and those who do not conform are vilified. Your groups exist only by creating the categories of us and them, the ally and the enemy. To accomplish this, groups play on two of your most powerful fears, fear of rejection and fear of not being accepted (two sides of the same coin). In short, your societies exist through fear. They vilify and debase the individual with fear. If individuals buy into the rules of this game they are rewarded with approbation and honors. If they refuse to play the game they are met with disapprobation, dishonor, calumny and rejection. The group sets up the individual for frustration and anger, winners and losers and success and failure. Your complex societies are awful entities and the bane of your little minds.

But there is more to the story. As your societies become more complex they subdivide into social groups, divisions and classes. These divisions often are based on race, gender, age, class and wealth. In your most highly evolved and complex societies the division creates rigid castes and hereditary aristocracies. Other animals have no similar societal divisions. A pack of wolves, for example, may have a natural hierarchy based on strength and fierceness but unlike you it has no divisions based on ancestry, wealth, education and employment. Your societal constructs ossify divisions and freeze your natural differences through laws, institutions, customs and morality.

This is what happens when you endeavor to undo and rearrange my patterns of nature. The irony is that you have rejected my natural divisions but fixed these artificial divisions with your construct of society. And the entrenchment of these divisions causes you so many problems. They are responsible for most disagreements, including wars, revolutions, insurrections and rebellions. As these divisions increase your societies further fractionalize into ideologies that support a particular group's viewpoint such as your political parties. This fragmentation increases with creation of low, middle and high-class societal strata. It is a long story but this fragmentation destroys your societies. Your historians Mr. Gibbon and Mr. Toynbee pointed this out. The common reason for decay and destruction of your past societies has been division and internal discord. I do not have to explain further. All you need do is read your own history books to understand this phenomenon.

Your stratification by class exists only because you created this artificial construct of society. Nature has no similar classes and the other animals have no such entrenched divisions. Your highest class, or aristocracies and their self-proclaimed "high society" so conspicuously demonstrate the artificial nature of your societies. The very idea of high society would not exist if you had not created the concept of society. It truly is the unicorn offspring of unicorn parents. Pretenders to high society live in a make-believe world of their imagination. The entrance requirements are vague and ethereal. They may be based on wealth, ancestry, who you know, who likes you or where you went to school. Membership often depends on one's conviviality and wit, ability to comply and copy or aptitude at being a sycophantic toady. Merit rarely factors into the entrance requirements. High society is fickle and one's fate ultimately depends on others' feelings or the winds of caprice. It is a fluid, ethereal, fey, gossamer and illusionary entity where reputations hang on opinion, gossip, rumor and innuendo. You are never quite sure whether you or others are in it. As your Mr. Adams once said, your societies have no unity; you wander about them like a maggot in cheese. Despite this, members of high societies jealousy defend their status vigilantly trying to preserve their imaginary position. Because it is just a manifestation of your imagination high society lacks foundation and is just a game you play.

The Nature of Relationships

Your civilizing constructs, like your societies, have made your lives a script that requires you to play multifaceted roles. I must admit that your script entertains me—I do enjoy tragedies. But I am amazed at how many relationships are written into the script as well as your ability to perform the incredibly complex roles each demands. Your scripts have made you citizens, patients, plaintiffs, mortgagees, presidents, tenants, wives, parishioners, taxpayers, constituents, students, employees, clerks, licensees, bureaucrats, and clients. The list is endless. You have created so many relationships and roles for yourselves that your lives have become agonizingly complex, convoluted and difficult. Much of your lives are spent endeavoring to navigate these numerous and varied script relationships. Other animals have few similar relationships and roles, which makes their lives far more simple and natural.

A few natural relationships exist along with a panoply of unnatural ones that you created. Your natural ones are primarily with each other and derive from your instincts to reproduce and survive. For example, two natural include the love relationship between different genders and the parent-child relationship. The love relationship is obvious. It comes from your instinct to reproduce and manifests itself mainly as lust. It compels you to procreate. The parent-child relationship derives primarily from your instinct to survive. It manifests itself as nurturing which insures the survival of your offspring and species. These natural relationships and roles are primitive and necessary connections that fulfill your instincts.

Pretty simple so far, but you have made it incredibly convoluted.

Your imagination and constructs have created so many additional unnatural relationships and roles that keeping them straight is hard. These relationships occur between yourselves or between individuals and your constructs. They all are products of your imagination. Marriage, for example, creates husband and wife, government creates state and citizen, religion creates priest and parishioner, law creates defendant and plaintiff, society creates low and upper classes, economic systems create creditor and debtor and sexual proclivities create prostitute and John. None of these unnatural relationships exists in nature. Other animals do not have husbands and wives, states and citizens, priests and parishioners, defendants and plaintiffs, upper and lower classes, creditors and debtors or prostitutes and Johns. If you had not created the idea of a state, for example, then you never would have a citizen or taxpayer or the roles they demand. If you had not created these entities the resulting relationships, as well as the roles, simply would not exist.

As I discussed earlier, you are a naturally selfish and aggressive creature. Therefore, for these relationships and roles to function your selfishness and aggressiveness must be suppressed, truncated, and delimited. You must constantly sublimate you personal interests and suppress your aggressiveness to maintain these relationships and fulfill the roles they require. This makes conspicuous the very unnatural and artificial nature of these obligations because they run counter to your human natures. Because suppressing your natures is difficult these relationships are frail and often fail when your selfishness and aggressiveness prevail. To appreciate this, just observe the fickleness of your relationships. Never perfect, they come and go, your ability to maintain them always fluctuates and the value you give them goes up or down. Your relationships, such as friendships, marriages and creditor-debtor are constantly forming, changing, and failing. And when they fail you fail at the roles they demand.

What you have done is pit your selfish and aggressive human natures against what you created. You naturally resist the oppressive and pervasive obligations and duties that these relationships and roles impose. They force you into numerous complex, obligatory and duty-filled situations that you resent. They make many of you very angry and resentful spouses, taxpayers, Protestants, revolutionaries, anarchists, proletariats, criminals and debtors. This, of course, causes much of your interpersonal and extra-personal conflict, friction and violence.

This tension now extends even to your primitive and natural relationships. Once relatively peaceful natural relationships now are full of discord. So extended are the natural love and parent-child relationships that they now torment many of you. You have made the love relationship a marriage contract covering couples who chafe at the lifelong obligations and restrictions it imposes. You have turned the parent-child relationship into an eighteen-year rearing marathon with naturally rebellious teenagers. Many cannot tolerate these relationships and the roles they demand which is why so many marriages fail and teenagers struggle to free themselves from the parental yoke.

You have set the bar so high for relationships that many of you cannot fulfill the roles they demand. Some are more capable but eventually most of you fail. All you need do is look around at those who are divorced, outlawed, outcast, poor and licentious to realize how often you fail to fulfill these imposed, unrealistic relationship roles. In fact, virtually all your artificial roles are failing. Most of you simply do not have the diligence, cannot make the effort or lack the will to maintain them.

These failures greatly concern many of you. The main reason: if your relationships and roles fail so do your constructs. Your constructs will not function if you do not play the roles they require. For example, if you refuse to play the roles of husbands and wives your institution of marriage will quickly fail, or if you refuse to play citizen and taxpayer your construct of government will collapse. It truly is like your sage Mr. Shakespeare said: your lives are a stage, and you must act the roles for the play to go on.

I want to comment on one curious relationship of yours. Unlike the others, it does not directly derive from your survival and reproduction instincts. Nor is it a product of your constructs. It is friendship, one of your most lauded, misunderstood and significant relationships. Many of your thinkers and poets have commented on this unusual relationship. For example, your Mr. Lucretius the Epicurean said he simply wanted to sit with friends and live out his life enjoying beauty. Given your instincts, I was perplexed for a long time at the development of this relationship. It seemed that the qualities of friendship, such as kindness, tenderness and acceptance were not in keeping with your natures.

What I found is that this relationship is compatible with your natures and, if you think about it, quite natural. You simply misunderstand the nature of it. You think your friendships are altruistic but they are not because they are all about you, the individual. They appeal to your selfish natures because they make you feel good. You like others because they like YOU, you like them because they accept YOU, you like them because they are compatible with YOU and you like them because they honor YOU. You create friendships for innumerable reasons but the common factor is they are friends because of YOU and not them. If you doubt this ask yourselves how many friendships you form with those who dislike you, do not accept you or do not honor you. The truth is that your friendships are based on your selfishness, not altruism.

They fulfill your need to be liked, accepted, honored and entertained. They make you happy.

However, it is deeper than this. The significant and essential reason for your friendships is to give your lives meaning. Friends are refuges from the existential, meaningless void of reality. They are a connection that makes you feel not alone; they give you fellow journeymen. You take comfort, for example, in exchanging problems with your friends because it makes you feel like you are not alone facing these issues—someone else is also dealing with them. You take great comfort in knowing others also die. The beauty of your friendships, unlike all you other relationships and roles, is that they are truly symbiotic because each gains from the experience. They are voluntary and do not carry the tremendous obligations and duties of the other relationships.

The Role of Government

The most conspicuous manifestation of your civilizing efforts is your construct of government. It is a most curious concept. I have watched you develop it with utmost interest. I never envisioned what you call government; it came entirely from your imagination. A blessing and a curse, it helps and torments you. It is true that with government you curbed your naturally selfish and aggressive natures and in the process did some good. But it is also true that this entity has caused you considerable violence and suffering. If you think about it these governments of yours have killed, enslaved, subdued, taxed, coerced, forced, controlled, manipulated and reduced you. Ironically, you invented this entity for protection but used it to kill one another. It has institutionalized and magnified your violent natures. Because it organized you so broadly it has inflicted considerable damage to your species.

The first thing I noticed is that whenever you form a government it immediately begins appropriating your wealth. It takes the fruits of your labors and diminishes your most able citizens. You naturally work to acquire security for survival but your governments take this bounty with what you call taxes. Your Mr. Marx, a most disagreeable man, proposed that you use your construct of government to take according to ability and provide according to need. This is a most curious concept. It is the opposite of what I intended. In nature, the able survive and the least able perish. This is all part of the pattern. Instead, under his plan you punish your able and succor your least able. Your initial efforts with this unrealistic formula have all failed and I think that over time you will find it causes you innumerable unforeseen problems.

You keep trying to create the perfect government but all efforts fail. Someone is always left out of the equation. You cannot do it because your governments are artificial. You often use your ideals of freedom, justice and equality as criteria for creating governments as well as judging their goodness. But these ideals are themselves artificial, human-made, unnatural, contradictory and impossible to achieve. You will never create the perfect government.

These imaginary polities, or what your Mr. Burke called moral essences, do not naturally exist. You create these imaginary social entities and then ascribe to them nonexistent qualities. You imagine qualities like the social weal, and entities like the public that your governments purportedly embody. You then audaciously assume they grant all citizens certain rights and duties which they then are to superintend. You imagine, for example, that government is a partnership that ascribes duties between generations, between the living, the dead and the yet born. You ascribe rights such as the right to security, justice, and equality. But what you are really talking about is power and all you are really doing is describing and allocating it. And then, because these ideals do not exist you must make your governments coercive and powerful to implement what you have imagined. If these ideals of freedom, justice and equality existed naturally governments would not be needed to implement them. You are creating unnatural and unassailable ends that require some very pernicious and necessary means to achieve. These means are your tar pit. Ultimately, your imaginary rights and duties are about limiting individual freedom and taking from some to provide for others.

In spite of all your lofty talk about the functions and purposes of your concept of government they have become matters of who controls whom. They are about power, the power for some to control others. Your governments are essentially power struggles among yourselves; they are about controlling and being controlled. Your Mr. Aristotle unwittingly made this reality conspicuous with his classifications of government. He classified them based on who rules and their purpose. A single person conducts a monarchy for the public interest and a tyranny for his own private interests. In reality both the monarch and the tyrant rule for their own interests. Mr. Aristotle thought minorities conducted aristocracies for the public interest and oligarchies for their own interests. In reality, both rule for their own interests. Finally, he called polities states where the majority governs for the public interest and democracies where the majority rules for its own interests. In reality, the majority rules in its own interests in both cases. Your Mr. de Tocqueville called this the tyranny of the majority. Socialism is the extreme example of this where the majority poor plunder the minority rich. Your contemporary communistic form of government is an oligarchial tyranny because it outlaws other parties and allows no competition. Personally, I think all forms of your government are to some degree kakistocracies (government by the worst) or ochlocracies (government by the mob). Your history has shown that whoever rules invariably uses power to further their own interests. Your Mr. Hamilton said that when the minority rules it tyrannizes the majority and when the majority rules it tyrannizes the minority.

You do not understand that your concept of government has caused you to be increasingly controlled by other people rather than nature. Individual humans control your governments and you resist other individuals treating you arbitrarily, capriciously and unjustly. These people, through the coercive force of government, impose, limit, reduce, control and force you. You can accept nature's limits because you have little control over my design, but you chafe when controlled and directed by other people. Your wise Mr. Hayek wrote that you can endure the injustices caused by nature but not those caused by others of your species. You dislike being subject to the arbitrary power of another person or a majority's will.

Your concept of government came about for a number of reasons. The initial reason was your need to control your naturally selfish and aggressive natures. As I previously discussed your instinct to survive caused you to be inherently selfish and aggressive. Your aggressiveness is a virtue within the patterns of nature. It was essential for your survival and ability to reproduce. But you found that you often could accomplish more and live easier and happier lives together than alone. You found that doing so brought many conveniences such as rowads and sewers that your governments could provide more efficiently. But your governments made your aggressiveness a vice. You want to compete but this construct of yours required you to cooperate. To curb your aggressive nature you needed some coercive entity so you turned to government. Government was unavoidable because you had to curb your natural instincts to aggregate in peace. None of the other animals have government. They do have social organization but it is very different indeed. It reflects the animals' basic instincts but has no concepts like taxation or social weal and contains none of your ideals like justice or equality.

You also conceived of government out of fear. Without some form of control you found that your communities were unpredictable states of anarchy, danger, violence and chaos. You inherently fear the unknown and unpredictable. This is easily explained. If things are unknown your survival is threatened. Knowledge and predictability enhance your survival. The other animals naturally want to know as much as they can about what threatens them, including their environment and enemies. They want to know how others will act. Anarchy and unpredictability are danger to you and naturally cause you fear. You prefer to live with what you can predict so one reason you developed the idea of government was to make your circumstances more certain. This is why you often endure such awful governments. Your Mr. Shakespeare expressed this best-he wrote that you prefer to live with those troubles you know than those you know not of.

Many of your most imaginative and clever thinkers have pondered what constitutes your best form of government. Mr. Locke was very original when he proposed that government derives its authority from those it governs. Your Mr. Rousseau, like Mr. Locke, also envisioned your government being of the people but added an interesting little twist to your yarn. He proposed that you form governments from social contracts where everyone willingly gives up freedom for security. This idea, by the way, is about as close to my design as you can get because it is based on your selfishness. Mr. Hobbes added that a sovereign who he called Leviathan is needed to enforce this contract.

Your Mr. Locke also envisioned certain natural rights for each of you. He imagined your rights to life, liberty and property. Let me assure that in nature none of these rights exist. These are just things you want. Your imaginary rights are thin air, nonexistent and built on stilts as your Jeremy Bentham explained. Rights only exist because you created the construct of government. The only reason you created rights was to protect yourself from government which makes them negative. You only need the idea of a right because you created the concept of a government. There are no governments in nature and therefore no need for your concept of rights. In nature there are no rights.

Your Mr. Jefferson borrowed Mr. Locke's negative rights because they protect you from intrusive government. His rights were embellished later in the American *Constitution* and *Bill of Rights* which were again all negative and included freedom of speech, religion and assembly. Under socialism I have noticed many of you have come to think of these rights as positive or something you are entitled to. Many are not satisfied with just the right to speech so they demand that the government provide them a microphone so they can be heard. You will find that these new positive rights will be the end of your rights because they conflict with other rights. One person's right to housing conflicts with another's right to keep their property. You will end up with an endless war of rights and ultimately no rights.

The quality of your governments depends very much on how much authority you give them because the more power they have the more their pejorative consequences are magnified. Your worst forms of government are those that become very powerful and coercive. I think your Mr. Marx's socialistic, and certainly your Mr. Lenin's communistic, forms of government fit this type. They are arbitrary, capricious, violate your own rules of law, and insult my patterns of nature. Your best forms are those with limited power that govern according to your human natures. Your constitutional democracies are perhaps the best example of this form. Your Mr. Jefferson and Mr. Madison must have consulted my Muses when they created the American *Constitution*, *Bill of Rights* and checks and balances. These ideas allowed the majority of you to rule without becoming excessively tyrannical. Unfortunately, some of your contemporary "progressive" liberal thinkers are endeavoring to undo this with their utopian ideologies.

Predictably, and unfortunately for you, your concept of government has caused one of your greatest problems, your wars. You have always had conflicts but never on the scale your governments have created. Your aggressive and naturally selfish natures cause wars' evils but your governments vastly magnify these qualities. They turn your small skirmishes and clan raids into worldwide conflagrations. There are many reasons for your wars. Perhaps the main one is conflict between your governments over territory. They fight endlessly over this issue. I never intended states to have territory; I intended you to be fluid. Your societies naturally are born, grow, mature and die. They expand and contract. Your governments rarely account for this reality and so you have wars. If, for example, state boundaries were fixed at early points in time then your English would have to leave your America because the Indians were there first. But then the Anglos of England would have to leave for Northern France because the Britons were there before them. But the Teutons would then have to migrate back to Russia because they had displaced the Anglos, and the Mongols would have to migrate back east and the Han tribes would have to return to China.

Of course, the Indians would also have to quit America because they displaced the prehistoric tribes. This, of course, is preposterous. And while I am at it, I wish your governments would stop going to war in my name. I do not sanction these wars and I do not appreciate being the purported reason for so much of your suffering.

Before we leave the topic of government, I want to say one thing—your very wise Mr. Burke warned you that using government for social engineering is destructive. He said your search for a perfect form of government would ultimately destroy government, a process you already see but conveniently ignore. He was wary of abstract reason and where it might take your imagination. He eschewed strict ideologies and millenarian thinking. He did not believe in sacrificing the present for the future or means to ends. He thought government should adjust to human nature and not human reasoning. He thought you should be governed in a way agreeable to your disposition and temper. He was right and you should heed his warnings. Your artificial governmental constructs should be small, limited and geared to rule according to your human natures. When you endeavor to impose rigid ideologies, like socialism and communism, onto yourselves all you do is suffer.

The Nature of the Law

Governments are your struggle for power and your laws are how you enforce that power. They are arbitrary and artificial sets of rules that you created for controlling others and enforcing your rules. Other animals have no such arbitrary sets of rules. Their laws are the laws of nature which are survival of the fittest and might makes right. Your laws are not in nature and if you imposed them on the other animals they all would be guilty. You use your laws to enforce and maintain your constructs through fear and punishment. Your Mr. Machiavelli, one of your maligned thinkers, wrote you have two ways to control behavior-love and fear. Love is preferable because compliance is voluntary and from your own will but you readily break this bond when circumstances are not in your interests. For him, fear is far more reliable because you fear punishment. Your laws control your behavior with fear. Without these legal threats of punishment your constructs would never work.

I have always found it so curious that you feel safe walking the streets of your cities because you believe these imaginary laws protect you. The truth is these laws are very fragile, they constantly fail and your sense of security is false. Your cities are plagued with murder, rape, robbery, gangs, fights, altercations and riots. Your laws are just ethereal ideas that disappear with the slightest breeze. Your flimsy civility depends entirely on your wills, your fear and your laws' ability to maintain them. Without these ideas of armor you are very dangerous animals to each other. You are like domesticated wild dogs that could revert to their original wild wolf states at any moment. Your violent natures, always just under the surface, are unpredictable and rear up under many capricious circumstances. You are walking time bombs just one step from violence. I have often wondered why you restrict the other animals with your zoos but not yourselves.

Originally, your law was based on creating peace. It was an agreement among yourselves, or contract, not to kill one another. This form of law worked reasonably well because it caused you to trust one another. Gradually, you conceived of the ideal of justice, which does not exist in nature, to enforce these social contracts. It formed the basis of your laws and the foundation of your trust. It is a concept that let you get along. This justice also caused you to imagine your concept of the rule of law requiring all to be treated equally. This allowed you to escape capricious and arbitrary rule by others. This form of law is what many of you call naturalistic law. It was the original and essential basis for your law. It arose naturally when you aggregated and when not carried to extreme it did a yeoman's job of maintaining your early constructs and enforcing your social contracts. It required, for example, that justice demand punishment for those who kill. These laws were the means to achieve your ends. You imagined desirable ends, such as safety, and then promulgated laws to achieve them.

Your ancient Mr. Cicero first described your naturalistic laws. He believed they derive from the timeless moral laws of nature, or from me. He believed your laws exist in nature and not in books and are higher than your human law. He thought your law and morality were one which meant that they must be based on justice. Another early proponent of this naturalistic law was your Mr. Aquinas who also distinguished between my eternal higher law and your temporal human law. Another proponent of your naturalistic law was Mr. Blackstone who reconfirmed that your laws were the realization of the moral laws of nature.

However, you encounter a problem with your naturalistic law. You use one of your imaginary ideas as a basis for your imaginary constructs. You imagined the concept of morality on which you base your construct of law. The problem is that your idea of morality does not exist in nature. There is no right or wrong in nature. You just imagine these moral laws to enforce your social contracts so you can live together in peace. Ultimately, your natural law based on morality will not work because you cannot define morality. Your imagination is attempting to base one system, your law, on another, your morality, which itself is indescribable and unexplainable. I will say that your natural law worked about as well as any of your artificial constructs could. It engendered trust, enforced your social contracts and allowed you more peace than you had in nature.

But then a subtle shift occurred in your law. Your laws have two aspects which are to restrict and compel. Your naturalistic law emphasizes restricting your behaviors more than compelling them. Your restrictive laws tend to forbear individuals' conduct, so, for example, they do not kill or steal. They are essentially negative. This form is very similar to nature's laws which also tend to restrict behavior. But as your constructs became more elaborate you started using law to compel which commenced many of the problems with the law that you experience today. Your compelling laws require more than forbearance because they are have become mostly affirmative. They make you do something. Most of you can tolerate laws that restrict but chafe at those that compel. You can accept those laws that punish bad behavior but resent those that require good behavior. It is easier to tolerate a law that prevents you from doing what you have not done than a law that compels you to do what you do not want to do. Put another way, you naturally resist that which endeavors to recreate your nature. It is one thing, for example, to prevent someone from committing murder and entirely another to compel someone to redistribute the fruits of their labors.

This need to compel dramatically changed things. To re-engineer your human natures to conform to your constructs you conceived of what you call positivistic law. This new idea, which your Mr. Bentham and Mr. Hobbes promoted, detached your law from morality. They described your laws as just your creations or social facts that enforce social norms. They do not distinguish right from wrong or turn an "is" into a "ought." They are just commands to obey. This was the beginning of the end for your construct of law. You began basing laws on your Mr. Bentham's utilitarianism, or happiness for the most, and compelling yourselves to achieve that end. Ironically, you unwittingly commenced the process of destroying what made your laws work. When you detached your laws from right and wrong you lost your concept of justice. When you decided, for example, that justice demanded that those in need should be provided for by others you began committing injustice to those others. You cannot derive justice from injustice. What your positivistic laws do is broker power.

With this new concept of law your problems started compounding. You found that your new positivistic utilitarian laws conflicted, violated you concept of justice, violated your social contracts, destroyed trust and became increasingly arbitrary and capricious. Your legal systems began breaking down because they were groundless. The only way you could resolve these conflicts was for individuals to make arbitrary decisions to resolve disputes. These individuals were your judges and what you call realistic law was the solution. You began letting the judges decide.

Your Mr. Holmes and Mr. Douglas championed this new legal manifestation of your imagination. They claimed that to understand the law you should watch what your judges do. They said that because you have so many laws on the books your judges could literally support whatever result they want. Consequently, they reasoned that understanding how judges make decisions ultimately defines what law is. This made law a social science because many things influences judges such as ideology, politics, economics, sociology, parentage and their last meal. So, to understand your law you had to study these things. But this just made your law free-floating and subjective. It became more groundless. Resolutions of your disputes no longer were based on justice or even happiness for the most but rather expedience and improvisation. This has resulted in some very absurd and mischievous consequences.

You have made your law like a game where the scorer arbitrarily makes the decisions about the score without following any written rules. I think your Mr. Douglas said he did not follow precedent but rather made it. This comment could just as easily come from one of your despotic rulers. Now you are getting different interpretations of the score, conflicting results and no fair or just game. Your law is increasingly unpredictable because there are no more rules. Instead, your laws are what one judge says they are. What you write down as law, or intend as law is meaningless and your constitutions are becoming only what judges say they are. Indeed, your Mr. Bishop Holiday once wrote;

Nay whoever hath an absolute authority to interpret any written or spoken laws it is he who is the lawgiver to all intents and purposes and not the person who first wrote or spake them.

It should come as no surprise then that in your more advanced societies' legal systems the most contentious issue is who the judges are. They, in effect, become your rulers. To make society conform to your worldview you must now select judges who share your perspective. Predictably, your selection of judges has become very contentious.

The upshot of all this is that your imagination increasingly makes your laws meaningless. They are not grounded, they do not enforce your social contracts, they are unpredictable and many of you no longer trust them. They are increasingly arbitrary, capricious, and violate your rule of law. Ironically, you are now returning to the state in nature where you began. A state of anarchy and chaos where might makes right and you are unsafe. You originated the problem with natural law, compounded it with positivistic law and then tried to cover it up with realistic law. What irritates me is that you now blame me because there is no justice in the world. Humans, you are a strange duck indeed.

The Nature of Politics

I do not want to talk long on this topic because, frankly, I disdain your politics and your politicians. They are a consequence of your cleverness and one of your worst developments. Your politics are utilitarian in nature and all about expediency. They are a computing system and not a moralizing one. They are not about truth or goodness; they are about what works. Your politics do not make you better, they only enable you to coexist in peace. I find them ignoble, dissembling, malevolent, ungrounded and slimy.

Your politics occurred because you used your imagination to conceive of a better world. To achieve this better world you developed certain concepts that implemented this vision. But your imagination is not good enough to envision something perfect so your concepts are not perfect which makes you imperfect within your conceptual constructs. You are imperfect within them because they remove you from my patterns. My patterns, on the other hand, are perfect and within them you are perfect. Your politics arose because you needed something to soothe the problems caused by these imperfect and imaginary constructs. In nature your politics play no part.

Your constructs require you to collectivize and your politics are the natural result. Put another way, you could never collectivize without politics which means that without politics your constructs would never work. Further, due to the exegesis of these structures the bigger they get the greater your need for politics. The further you get from my patterns the more you separate yourselves from your essential natures and the more contentious you become. Your solution of choice has been politics, a process that placates you. It subdues you by soothing friction, compromising and facilitating. It is an unctuous and serpentine process intended to persuade you that you want what you do not want and to do what you do not want to do.

The bigger your constructs the more the combatants and the more you need politics. These immense structures and imaginary creations are virtual breeding grounds for conflict and enemies. To ameliorate this trend in some of your more advanced societies you developed the idea of diversity which only brought you more friction, division and more enemies. What's more, these are artificial enemies. They do not occur in nature, they only occur because you created them. And to top it off, these bigger constructs that created heretofore-unknown enemies exponentially inflame your hatreds, which require even more of your politics to referee and superintend. It was your own Mr. Adams said politics is the organization of hatreds. These hatreds are everywhere. You see them not only between yourselves but also between you and your constructs. Your artificial ideas develop concepts like wealth, money, and ownership which pit rich versus poor; and governments, which pit those with power and the ability to compel against those without power.

Other concepts springing from your artificial ideas are laws, which make some of you lawbreakers and others law obeyers, religion, which pits theists against atheists, and morality, which pits those with virtue against those with vice.

But you have created even more combatants. Your constructional paradigms require you to collectivize which has pitted the individual against the collective group. As an individual you forever conflict with your societies. Your societies respond by compelling you to cooperate which you as individuals naturally resist. Your social systems have become increasingly inimical to your human natures. Simply read one of your history books to observe that you are forever battling your governments, your laws, your ethics and your religions. And if all this is not bad enough your artificial constructs themselves have become enemies. As I mentioned earlier, because they are products of your imagination they are all different so they commence fighting among themselves to see which is best or who controls whom. You see this all the time. Your states, societies, and religions, for example, are always sparring and at odds. I am explaining all this because you now see why your politics are so necessary. They had to develop to keep peace between all of the enemies that you created.

This demonstrates that your politics are essentially about power, or the power to make your artificial constructs function. They are necessary because they compel the implementation of your artificial ideas and enable your social organizational systems to function. Without this power to compel these entities could not exist. Politics is also about the allocation of power. Those who get power are free and those who do not are not free. One group is the free compeller and the other the controlled compelled. Nature has no politics or politicians because the other animals do not have your cleverness.

Your politics are artificial and empty; they solve nothing other than to enable you to get along. They are a compromising process that uses your artificial ideals of freedom and justice to control you when in reality these ideals lose out to utility. Your politics is a base, crude and expedient prerequisite for your cooperation. If you do not believe me just observe what happens when your politics fail. You quickly engage in all forms of conflict including insurrection, rebellion, revolution and war. Indeed, your own Carl von Clausewitz once wrote that politics is just war by other means.

In many respects politics represents the failure of your constructs. You envision a better world with your invention of government, law, morality, religion and society, but these cannot function without politics. You must compromise these constructs with your politics which just compromises the better world you envisioned. If these constructs were natural and perfect then your politics would not be necessary. Only because they are artificial is political power required. You must appreciate the irony. You devised these constructs to prevent arbitrary coercion and intimidation but now are coerced, compromised and intimidated by your own politics and politicians. You have returned to that utilitarian, coercive, arbitrary, intimidating and capricious state you endeavored to escape.

The only thing worse than your politics is your politicians, or those who superintend your politics. In your simple states, like your early America, statesmen such as Mr. Washington led your government. Because this governmental construct was small there was little power to attract the politicians. These kinds of individuals were motivated primarily by the welfare of the state and you called them statesmen. But as your states grew the more powerful and coercive exerted themselves—your politicians. Self-interest primarily motivates them. They are the opportunists and manipulators among you. They have mastered the art of political talking without meaning, they usually do not know what they say, what they say seeks to proselytize and their goal is power.

Consider, for example, how your politicians seize control of governments. They appeal to your selfish interests, promise you things you want (which are usually things they cannot deliver) and take control of your futures. Those politicians capable of offering the most alluring and compelling future vision, the one that appeases your selfish interests, get the power. Power always flows to those politicians who grab possession of your futures. Your politics and politicians truly are necessary evils created by your imaginary and unrealistic constructs.

The Nature of Morality

Some of you, like your ancient Mr. Aquinas, claim that a timeless and universal natural morality exists. They claim that I gave you certain rules by which to live your lives. Let me set the record straight: I did no such thing. What I gave you was a set of circumstances, or patterns, within which you live. From these circumstances certain rules of behavior logically arose which you call morals. You could call these rules natural because they occur due to circumstances but ultimately they are entirely of your making. They are a consequence, like your other constructs, of you imagination. As I discussed in my opening remarks, you promulgate these moral rules because they enhance your safety and survivability when you aggregate. They enforce your original social contracts. Your Mr. Hume called them sentiments or your opinion of the way you want to act. He was right—you made these moral rules so they are not in nature.

You had to create these rules of morality because you are essentially selfish creatures. You resist cooperation in nature when it is not in your interests so (similar to your laws) you had to develop some form of coercion for your moral constructs to function. That coercion, which enforced your moral rules, was achieved through social approbation and disapprobation. You found that this worked pretty well because you naturally like to be accepted. Curiously, acceptance and rejection are two of your greatest fears. They also were more fluid and less severe than laws that enabled you to control a greater range of your behaviors. The other animals have no such moral systems of right and wrong and no need for moral approbation and disapprobation because there is no morality in nature.

Your original moral rules were embodied in your religions such as the Ten Commandments which you think I gave you. They included rules against killing, committing adultery, stealing, lying and being envious. They were quite practical because they enforced your contracts which allowed you to live in peace. You decreed that those adhering to these commandments were moral and had virtue while those who did not were immoral and had vice. What quaint ideas, vice and virtue. Imagine telling a monkey that he has no virtue because he steals or a jackal that he has vice because he kills. They would just look at you and wonder what you are talking about. Anyhow, in your case, you call ethical those capable of controlling their natures and adhering to these rules and you call unethical, unprincipled and immoral those incapable of controlling their natures. Your clever priests used this morality to gain power. They began claiming if you were immoral then you were evil. They intended this proselytizing to instill fear in you. For them it is all about power. By the way, I wish you had not made me the object of the rest of your Ten Commandments. Your attention flatters me but it is unnecessary and only causes you a lot of confusion.

Some of you may ask why not just make these rules laws and dispense with the morality? The reason is because your selfish natures make you obstreperous and contumacious little shits who strenuously resist being told what to do. You found that when you make these rules laws you create too many lawbreakers. You discovered that you could not legislate morality. You found that your constructs were succored with flexible rules that guided behavior, rules that gave individuals the opportunity to follow them voluntarily. In this respect your morals are a middle ground between law and anarchy. They are the glue the holds your constructs together because they do not carry the coercive power of your laws. Because they are voluntary the only sanctions are social disapprobation and shame. Many endeavor to escape this morality and you call them libertines.

For these moral rules to work, you had to create the concepts of personal responsibility and accountability. You had to hold individuals responsible for violating your rules. I am sure by now you see that there is no personal responsibility or accountability in nature. The other animals kill, commit adultery, steal, dissemble and covet all the time and there are no consequences. For you and your constructs, however, these concepts were necessary because they enabled you to live better lives by enforcing your social contracts. When you are virtuous then others refrained from killing you, stealing from you, taking your spouse and lying to you. Your ancient Greeks called this happiness through virtue or eumoirous which is based on the idea that if you treat others well they will treat you well. Some of your religions call this the golden rule. Note that this rule is based on your self-interest admonishing you to do unto others how YOU want them to treat YOU and not how the other wants you to treat them. You even have the proverb that says, "Old sins cast long shadows" and a poem that goes something like this:

> Our sins, like our shadows,
> When our day is in its glorie scarce appear.
> Towards our evening
> How great and monstrous they are

Your poets are such an unusual breed. I find them fascinating. They always try to express the inexpressible. Most of them struggle because what they want to express really is inexpressible. They cannot express it because it does not exist. Most endeavor to describe your vestigial emotions but their imagination extends the feelings so far that they end up trying to capture what has dissipated like smoke in a strong breeze. They are attempting to express that which no longer has form.

Anyhow, back to our topic. These morals of yours thwart your natural instincts and your instincts are powerful indeed. Morality then comes down to two things, the strength of your desires and the strength of your will. Put simply, the most moral among you are the most successful at thwarting their human natures. They have the weakest desires and strongest wills. The immoral have the strongest desires and the weakest wills which makes your morality willpower. In the end, your morality is only as good as your ability to suppress your instincts.

This shows that your morality, like your other constructs, requires some coercion. You must evoke social disapprobation and shame to enforce the rules. This puts you at war with yourself. You want the rules but do not like how they must be employed. You especially do no like to be shamed. I found your Mr. Hawthorne's book, *The Scarlet Letter*, ironic. On one hand, the society he describes endeavors to control sexual behavior for obvious reasons but on the other he derides this effort to control. You want to control behavior but do not like what accomplishes it.

Your biggest problem with morality occurs when your imagination gets carried away and you begin using morality in draconian ways to maintain your increasingly complex societal organizations. You stray from their original purpose, which was enforcing your social contracts, and implement rules inimical to your instincts. You begin calling compassion and altruism virtues and selfishness and self-interest vices. This development puts you squarely at odds with your selfish human natures. You begin violating your social contracts because these "higher morals" are unilateral. They are no longer mutual agreements but rather enforced unilateral decrees. Most of you obey them reluctantly. The predictable result is that your advanced civilizations require increasing amounts of disapprobation and coercion to function as a construct.

Your morality is just one big cycle and you are like a rat endlessly running in a wheel that goes nowhere. Your wheel begins turning when you create moral rules to enforce your social contracts which you call civilization. But then your imagination starts breaking down morality and you forget why you created it in the first place. As you forget the rules your natural passions engage and you commence dissipating your rules. As your advanced civilizations attenuate your morality you begin returning to your natural state, like the other animals. You call this decadence because it represents the decay of your moral rules. As your decadence increases the problems that your morality was intended to correct reappear reminding you why you created the rules in the first place. Then it starts over again and you re-establish and reinforce your morality. At least the rat gets some exercise.

The Nature of Language

Your imagination gave birth to your metaphysical speculations and your language gave them life. Your original language was simple like that of the other animals. This natural language arose within the patterns of nature and communicated simple messages like warnings, directions and your basic emotional instincts. However, unlike the other animals, your imagination took over and created an unnatural language construct which exists outside nature's patterns. You invented this language to communicate the complex ideas that your imagination generates such as state, fate, sublimity and the rule of law. This language designates nothing in reality. Predictably, it totally confuses and confounds you. The other animals do not have your cleverness, do not envision your constructs and therefore do not have your unnatural language. They do not need words like government because they have no construct of government. They do not need words like fate because they do not have the concepts of free will and determinism.

Two of your eminent thinkers on the subject explained why your unnatural language confounds you. Your Mr. Locke said simple ideas only come from the impressions that objects make on your minds and complex ideas are just mixtures of these simple ideas. Consequently, the complex ideas that you build from these simple ideas are just arbitrary. They exist outside nature's patterns and do not refer to any real existence. Your Mr. Berkeley also thought these complex ideas were imperfect contrivances of your minds. He called them abstract ideas. According to him, most of your language problems occur because these abstract ideas signify nothing in particular in reality. As a result, both these thinkers believed your language caused innumerable errors, difficulties and misunderstandings in your knowledge.

Your unnatural language primarily confuses you two ways. First, as these thinkers explained, many of your words simply do not signify anything in reality. It is a hierarchy of confusion in language. At the base are simple words like yellow that refer to something. The color yellow cannot be reduced into smaller components, it just is. This is your simple and natural language. But then you begin imagining unreal things and creating complex words for them which is the genesis of your unnatural language. For example, you conceive of the concept of matter and then create the word to signify it. But what exactly is matter? When you attempt to describe it you always end up describing something else like hardness, extension or color. But these are just qualities of a thing and not the thing itself. Then you get frustrated and start describing atoms, neutrons, protons and electrons, but these are just other words for matter. So you then have to start all over and describe the qualities of atoms. And so it goes ad infinitum. You are never quite able to capture the nature of what you call matter. You think you know what it is but cannot explain it clearly and definitively.

You cannot explain it because your word 'matter' ultimately refers to nothing.

But it gets a lot more confusing. You begin imagining things beyond your experience and naming them. You can touch matter but not ideas such as justice and fate. These are just ideas in your minds signified by words you create. It is like building one of your tree houses without a tree. Then you compound this confusion by building your artificial constructs from these artificial words. Your governments, for example, become based on justice. But now you have two artificial things-your words and your constructs. You have your imaginary government as well as the word justice that is one of its characteristics. Then you begin building on this never-never construct land of language with the word and construct feeding on each other. It is like the relationship between the word unicorn and the characteristics of a unicorn. You claim animals with one horn and four legs are called unicorns and then proceed to describe the characteristics of herds of unicorns. Obviously, the problem is that none of these entities exists. It is no wonder you cannot agree among yourselves on the nature of your constructs, on the words that signify them or on the characteristics of a herd of unicorns. The result is massive confusion and misunderstanding.

This leads to another problem—you cannot agree among yourselves what these imaginary words mean. Consent is achieved only when each of you uses the same words and sees the same mental picture attached to them. But you cannot because these unnatural words are simply products of your capricious imaginations.

Each of you imagines different things so most of you have different connotations for the same word. You are simply incapable of holding the exact definition for the same word at the same time and know whether other people agree with your interpretation. This, as you might imagine, is the greatest source of your confusion and the foremost reason for your conflicts. In the end, misunderstanding and miscommunication cause most of your divorces, insurrections, revolutions, wars and failed relationships.

One consequence of this is you resort to metaphors, similes and analogies when your words fail you. Because you cannot say or agree what something is you say what it is like. Or you resort to verse rather than straightforward prose. Many of you claim that you are expressing truth when you say something is like something else. But all this does is increase your confusion because you are not communicating truth. Why confuse things by saying something is like something else? Why not just say what that something is? And if you cannot say what something is then are you really saying anything at all? Your metaphors confuse you because they do not always refer to things in reality and when they do you often cannot agree among yourselves on their meaning.

Poetry is the most extreme form of your metaphoric language. Many of you think this is your highest and best form of communication when in reality it is your most unnatural and confusing language construct. Think of what you are really doing in poetry. You see an object like a beautiful landscape, it excites certain emotions, which you interpret in poetic words and then describe as like something else. Then someone else reads your words, reinterprets what that something else is. This gives rise to their feelings which they then project onto the landscape object you observed in the first place. This process involved seven different layers of interpretation. You see it, get a feeling, interpret the feeling, translate this feeling into metaphor, another person reads your metaphor, which they reinterpret, which gives them a feeling which they then describe. This whole process is like making and breaking code. Why make communication code? Why make it so complicated? Why not just tell them to look at the landscape object and experience it directly?

When your imagination and feelings take over they cause many of you to develop different interpretations of the same impression, event or idea. Predictably, different people then get different impressions and metaphors for the same event. Some people interpret the landscape object one way and others another. This manifests itself in your unnatural language construct which makes it imperfect because few agree on the meanings of things. Your imagination manufactures your descriptions and is embodied in words whose definition nobody agrees on.

The chief purpose of you language is communication. When simple and drawn from your experience it communicates truth within the laws of nature. When complex it originates from your metaphysical speculations and exceeds my patterns-it becomes untruth and loses its ability to communicate accurately and uniformly. Your imagination causes language-dust and you cannot see. Thanks to your language you now all live in tree houses without the tree surrounded by haze.

Economics

The consequences of your cleverness are most evident in your endless meddling with your economies. You constantly tinker, manipulate and alter your economies to solve one problem but all you get are two more. You seem constitutionally incapable of leaving well enough alone. You may recall your Mr. Smith's explanation of your original, natural and uncontrolled economy. A spontaneously evolved economic pattern that consists of markets, bartering, negotiations and exchanging. It is a natural system because it is based on your instinctually selfish natures. It balances supply and demand, allocates resources, increases production of the things you want and need and keeps your population under control. This wonderful system has succored the health and wealth of your communities and enhanced your survivability. This is your natural economy because it operates within the patterns of nature.

But it was not good enough for you. Many of you do not like my natural economy because it offers no security and is often unpredictable. Above all, many object to it because it makes some wealthy which incites envy. So you fiddled with this natural economy and created controlled economies mostly through your states. The results are some very strange, hydra-like artificial and imaginary economic constructs that utterly defy one's imagination. And predictably they cause you a lot of problems.

You have contrived and developed many controlled and unnatural construct economies during your short time on Earth. Your ancient Rome and early feudal economic system are examples. However, your contemporary socialism particularly stands out. This new construct of yours demonstrates most clearly the problems of your unnatural economies. Your Mr. Marx's socialism is state control of the means of production and distribution of wealth according to the principle "from each his ability to each his need." As one of your most artificial economic systems it exists in various forms in virtually all your contemporary governmental and legal constructs. In your natural economy the individual controlled production and distribution but your socialism changed that.

You created socialism because of your survival instinct. You desire security to survive so you devised this system. To achieve it you had to equalize wealth and pull your most capable people back into the pack. You had to transfer some individuals' superior ability to survive to those less capable. You created, for example, governmental social programs for the less able and paid for them with taxes on those more able. In short, you force the redistribution of wealth to equalize survivability. You detach yourselves from the economic pattern in nature by taking away control of production and distribution from the individual and giving it to the state. What you found, however, is that every time your socialism solves one economic problem two more show up. Consequently, you now have socialistic economies full of problems, contradictions and ironies. Let me explain.

You thought socialism would bring economic freedom but found you could only do this by taking freedom. You purport to bring freedom to the less able but instead take freedom from the more able. What you really got was some temporary security for some and a totalitarian state for all. You exchanged freedom for a little security and in the process got tyranny and loss of your individuality. To function your socialism requires each of you to act like an ant in an ant colony subordinating individual interests to the collective colony. This development set the demands of your imaginary construct socialism against your instinctual selfishness and the result has been loss of incentive and individual freedom and, ironically, less security. Your natural economies succeeded because they rewarded effort while your socialism does the opposite. It punishes effort by taking from the most able and rewards indolence by providing according to need. You thought providing according to need was moral but discovered it was immoral because it eliminated consequences, attenuated personal responsibility and weakened accountability. You thought it would bring security for all but all you got was less security as your socialistic states' wealth inevitably declined. You also got more dependence and too many people because more survived.

Overpopulation brought on by socialism is a serious problem of yours. It the greatest threat to your survivability. Originally, nature could provide for you because you were few in number. Scarcity kept your population in balance, a reality explained by your unfairly maligned Mr. Malthus. However, your contrived economies and monopolistic states have changed all this so you are now overpopulating your planet. You are thwarting the patterns, increasing your numbers and fouling your nest. This is a very dangerous and self-destructive development brought on by your cleverness. Unless corrected it will eventually bring your extinction as a species. Devoting your energies to figuring out how to balance your population with your environment would be far more productive than solving how to feed everyone.

Besides overpopulation your unrealistic and artificial economic construct of socialism brought you injustice. You thought you could bring about "social justice," but you had to commit injustice to some in order to bring "justice" to others. But your justice is not justice unless it is just for all. You committed what you intended to prevent. You also appealed to other some of your other ideals like freedom and equality but all you got were the same problems. To achieve freedom and equality for some you had to limit others' freedoms and discriminate. You found that you could only achieve your economic construct of socialism by applying your ideals selectively. What you are really doing is endeavoring to use your imaginary ideals to make survival a right. You claim that your ideals of freedom, justice and equality grant you the right to survive. Of course in nature there is no right to survive.

Your socialism does not work because it is unrealistic. You are naturally an aggressive and selfish individual. Your aggressiveness makes you competitive and your selfishness makes you want to accumulate. Socialism requires you to act in opposition to these instincts. For it to function freely and voluntarily you must cooperate and be altruistic. But sometimes you don't want to cooperate so coercion is the only way you can bring about and maintain socialism. Your natural economy requires no coercion, it just spontaneously occurs. Needless to say, no socialism exists in nature and the other animals do not give according to ability or receive according to need. Instead, nature rewards ability and is indifferent to need.

Some of you point to one of my ant colonies to prove that you have a natural form of cooperative economic organization like socialism. But you are not ants. Unlike the ants you are clever which causes you to resist the ants' preordained fate. You are unique in that you question the legitimacy and authority of externally imposed obligations, duties and responsibilities-especially those imposed by other people. You are naturally skeptical of your man-made waffle iron constructs like socialism. I think your renowned ant specialist. Mr. E. O. Wilson summed it up best when he said about your socialism: nice theory, wrong species.

IV

GOD'S OBSERVATIONS ON HUMAN'S METAPHYSICAL SPECULATIONS

Your metaphysical speculations have detached you from my natural order of things. Your cleverness has created such supranatural ideas and massive artificial structures, such as societies, state and civilization that you are separated from my patterns. But your imagination has caused you to go even further by conceiving fantastic beliefs that depict things the way they are not. Beliefs that literally have no connection with anything. You have ignored your Mr. William of Ockham's advice and persisted in your headlong dash into confusion. Ockham's Razor admonished you to believe the obvious. It says that what can be explained by the assumption of fewer things should not be vainly explained by the assumption of more things. You are rarely satisfied with obvious explanations. Instead, your cleverness prefers those that are extreme, esoteric and abstruse. Let me describe some of your fantastic metaphysical speculations. It is difficult because I am explaining what does not make sense to you. It is like trying to explain a dream or justify existence of a unicorn, but I will try.

The Nature of Knowledge

Only you question whether you are a brain in a vat. Only you ask whether you can trust your senses. Imagine a monkey pondering whether he is a brain in a vat. Monkeys do not, but you do. Only you have skeptics like your ancient Sextus Empiricus who believe you can never attain certain knowledge. A product of your cleverness, this skepticism utterly befuddles you. You think you should know things then question whether you know them. You conceive imaginary concepts like reality, truth, spirituality and purpose and then wonder if you really know them. You create artificial opposites such as right and wrong, vice and virtue, good and bad and true and false then wonder whether you can know which is which. You ask if you think or exist and then wonder how you can know for sure if you think and exist. You are like a dog chasing his tail going around and around with your metaphysical questioning.

Your philosophers fondly engage in this merry-go-round of knowing. They pursue knowledge, wonder what they know, wonder if what they know is true then ask how will they know if what they know is true. Only you wonder whether you can know and if it is true. The other animals are just concerned with knowing enough to survive and reproduce. You have senses, experience and memory like the other animals, but your cleverness causes you to think you should have some knowledge beyond these, some kind of meta-knowledge. You think you should know things that do not exist, things you imagine. But your imagination confuses you. To avoid this confusion and make your knowledge intelligible, you endeavor to unify your knowledge. You try to force everything you know to fit together. Indeed, many of your thinkers have said that your pursuit of knowledge is an effort to unify. But ask yourselves, why do you need to unify knowledge? No unity of knowledge is needed in nature because everything fits; nature is free of ambiguity and irony. Only you face the problem of unifying what you know because you created extra-natural fragmented entities.

Your metaphysical thinkers have endlessly contemplated this topic. It particularly interests them because without answers their efforts are pointless. Without certainty of knowledge they are forever cast as speculators and dreamers. Your Mr. Plato was entertaining with his claim that your knowledge is recollection. Your rationalists, like Mr. Descartes, imagined that you could attain knowledge by going into your libraries and just thinking rationally. He thought you could know just because you think. Your empiricists, like Mr. Hume, believed true knowledge came from your senses, and your idealists, beginning with Mr. Kant, thought knowledge was a combination of the two. Your efforts have become increasingly bizarre with your claims to deductive, inductive and *a priori* knowledge, as well as your justified true beliefs. It is virtually impossible for me to explain what is really going on. It would be like trying to explain to a monkey who cannot know why he does not know.

The true nature of your knowledge is best explained by metaphorically comparing it to a pyramid or raft. Your knowledge is built upon certain timeless and universal truths like the shape of a pyramid. Comprising the base are truths that support the entire pyramid. These truths are the patterns that you see in nature—they are what are true. This is certain knowledge. Your problems begin when your cleverness creates entities outside these patterns. It causes you to ask why, a question that introduces your speculations. There is no why in nature, it just is. These entities become your fanciful ideas, illusions and constructs which create the need for another type of coherentist knowledge. Think of a raft floating on an open sea. The integrity of the raft depends entirely on how well everything fits together. It has no foundation and no tethers to land. It only has coherence. It is, as your Mr. Neurath said like a ship at sea that sailors continually rebuild.

Your coherentist view of knowledge then becomes how well your ideas, illusions and constructs fit together. The better they fit the better this artificial knowledge is and the more your effort to unify advances. However, because these ideas are from your imagination they never square with the way things are. They are always untrue, they never fit and you are left forever juggling your jerry-rigged house of knowledge to achieve a better outcome. Your must continually rebuild your raft to make sense of things. The other animals have no need for coherentist knowledge. They intuitively trust their senses, memory and experiences. They have no imaginary constructs and therefore have no need for coherentist knowledge. They do not need to tie together artificial ideas and constructs because they have none. They are not clever like you.

Because you are a limited creature with limited understanding you cannot know these foundations to knowledge. It is like seeing the tip of an iceberg: you see the effects of the foundation, or the patterns but you are ignorant of what lies underwater out of view. You are a limited creature who will never know truth. If you could you would be me.

Because you will never know truth and because your artificial coherentist knowledge is flawed you create diversions to explain and justify your ignorance. Your imagination has worked overtime on this one. Your Mr. Freud postulated that you have an unconscious where he claimed true knowledge resides, a knowledge hidden from your view. Your frustrated Mr. Plato asked whether it is better to be a dissatisfied Socrates or a satisfied pig. Others have said you cannot understand because I work in mysterious ways. And your Mr. Erasmus threw in the towel with his exclamation that ignorance is bliss. The answers to these speculations are that you cannot know your unconscious, you do make yourselves a dissatisfied Socrates, my patterns are obvious and you are depressingly ignorant.

The Difference between Reality and Illusion

Because you can never know reality you are relegated to speculating about the true nature of things. The natural consequence of these speculations is you imaginatively construct answers. But these answers are not true because they are of your making. These false answers create an artificial, illusionary web of existence in which you cannot differentiate between the real and the unreal. You invest so much time and effort developing these constructs that you actually think they exist. You live in a self-constructed dream world that you think is real. You think your constructs like government, law, religion, civilization and morality are real but they are not. They are just things you created. You think that your language really refers to things like happiness, justice and truth but they too are figments of your imagination. You think the roles you have created for yourself like taxpayer, citizen and spouse are necessary but they are merely parts of a play you wrote and perform in. You have created all these things and they are nothing more than illusions. Needless to say, the other animals have no similar constructs, language or roles. They live within reality because they are not playwrights.

I have often referred in my observations to your bard Mr. Shakespeare because he elucidated this problem so admirably. He likened your lives to a play starring each of you as shadow actors. He said what you take for concrete reality is usually illusion and what you think is illusion is often real. Your lives, he wrote, are *the stuff dreams are made of*. Your imagination has created such an artificial and illusionary play for you to perform that you now never know when to trust your own mind. This is your dilemma: you cannot decipher what is more real-reality or the play. Reality has become your role-playing and what is real has become your illusion.

Consider how illusionary your lives are. You live in a virtual world of make believe. Your ideas, concepts and constructs have created a virtual flood of artificial roles, relationships, duties and obligations. You get up to a clock even though your body says sleep because you created something that measures time unrelated to the rhythms of nature. In the role of a parent you must superintend a rebellious teenager because you created a society so complex that childhood must be extended into adulthood. You go to a job you abhor because you created an economic system that demands your participation if you are to survive; at this job you are labeled an employee that must be managed which is an artificial relationship that arose from your economic system. You pay for lunch using an overdrawn credit card because your accounting system created the role of debtor. Back at the office, you work in fear because your competition is ahead of you due to the economic system's demand that you produce. At the end of the day you get a paycheck that measures your worth as an artificial employee because your economic accounting system must keep score. Your position in this economic system is determined by the amount of your paycheck and your wealth which itself is based on property deeds, bank accounts and paper money that you created but ultimately mean nothing. When you get home you go to church and listen to a sermon that tells you stories you invented and obligations you think I gave you, then you feel guilty from this sermon because the morality you created set moral standards you cannot achieve. You live under a government that you created and it promulgates artificial laws to control your behavior and make you do things you resent. As your governments grow they promulgate more coercive laws that are supposedly based on ideals you created like justice, freedom and equality—but do not exist. Then the society you created classifies you as a member of a certain class based on artificial criteria like your wealth, ancestry and education that have nothing to do with who you really are. Finally, in the evening you have sex with the same partner because you created the concept of monogamy and the institution of marriage even though you really want to be promiscuous. Your whole lives are this way. You have created this vast and complicated play with innumerable artificial roles you must learn and act out. These roles impart obligations, duties and responsibilities that you must successfully discharge and if you do not you are called a failure. Your whole lives are illusions and you do not even know it. No wonder most of you are neurotic. Of course the other animals have none of this. They just live.

What makes all this so interesting is that you are also a very judgmental animal. Each of you thinks you know what is right and true and thus constantly judges as wrong those who disagree with you. Each of you feels entitled to judge others' worth and value. These are more often not passive judgments but haughty and myopic decrees. But most of your judgments are wrong because your lives are illusions. You create false constructs then judge others' ability to adhere to them even though you cannot do so yourself. The imaginary constructs you created are false, the parts that these constructs created are false and your ability to judge is false because you can never know truth. What you are really doing is judging how well each of you acts the parts in your own play. It is like a blind person, who has never seen, judging how well another blind person sees.

Collectively, your illusionary existence becomes most conspicuous with your concepts of realism and idealism. You may recall that I discussed this topic earlier explaining that you imagine certain artificial ideals like justice and then act is if they are true. The consequence is constant tension between the way things are—reality—and the way you want things to be—the ideal. In truth, your ideals are just illusions perpetrated by your idealists. Consider, for example, your artificial construct of justice. Your idealists conceive of the concept of fairness, call it justice, and then develop endless reasons why it exists. They then use it to justify your construct of law. They say that all laws are to be fair and just. This may be a noble effort but it is illusionary. Your laws are not based on justice, they are essentially utilitarian in nature; they are about expedience. Try as you might you never quite achieve justice. It is like a mirage that always recedes as you draw near. It is always somewhere else and never where you are. Just examine the history of your law to appreciate how much might and not justice makes right in your legal systems. And to make matters worse you even disagree among yourselves over what the ideal of justice means.

Ask yourselves, how can you possibly base your legal systems on a concept whose meaning you cannot even agree on? The result causes you to say one thing (that laws are based on justice) and do another (make them utilitarian). So you live in this swirling world of legal illusion believing what is not true and doing what is false while believing it is all real.

As individuals your illusions are more personal. But you deceive yourselves in so many ways. You think you are noble but are base, you think you are moral but act immorally, you think you are good but do bad things and you think you are truthful but lie. The list is endless. You pray to false idols, trying to be what others want you to be or what your constructs demand, but rarely what you really are. Your ideas, ideals, traditions, constructs and customs enslave you by relegating you to live illusionary lives. The obvious consequence is that your lives are one continuous collision between what you want and the way things are. You are caught in a suspended state of tension between reality and illusion, unable to achieve any resolution. Your lives are just one damn thing after another. You are doomed to act out the roles you created in a tragic play that never ends.

The Significance of Death

Sorry, but you all die. Unlike other animals, however, circumstances have ensnared you in a cruel hoax. Your cleverness makes you aware that you die but you are not clever enough to understand what death is. As your Mr.

Nagel explained, none of you can conceive of nonexistence because you look at it from the inside, or from your side. You cannot conceive of annihilation or unconsciousness because your senses are unable to experience unconsciousness or annihilation. It is like you explaining time: you can only describe its effects but not time itself. Therefore, death is impenetrable for you (but not me). To escape this dilemma you just imagine what death is and make up what it is like. Your explanations are always wrong. Your thinkers on death are like brilliant mathematicians who always get the wrong answers.

I am sorry to be the bearer of news you think is bad but the truth is when you die you become nothing. You cease to exist and return to the elements. Death is just nothingness. It is nonexistence. Your body ceases to function and decays, your mind stops thinking and crumbles and you become worm food. Some propose that your mind, or consciousness, continues, but the truth is your mind's functions depend entirely on your biological body. When your body ceases to function so does your mind.

This nothingness really bothers you. It bothers you because you cannot comprehend it and what you cannot comprehend you usually fear. This fear drives much of your attitude about death. It is actually two fears, the fear of pain and the fear of the loss of experience. I cannot help you much with the pain because, as you say, shit happens. But your fear of losing experience is strange. If you think about it, having experience is stranger than having no experience. Being nothing is a lot easier than being something.

As a balm for your fear of death you have conceived very imaginative and sometimes fantastic nostrums. Your creativeness impresses me. Your primitive, superstitious societies were most imaginative when dealing with death. They conceived numerous fairytales to explain it. Many made you immortal. Your religious construct took it to a new level and conceived of a heaven and afterlife. I have news for you: there is no heaven but there is an afterlife—it is called dirt. Your ancient Epicureans, lead by your Mr. Epicurus, believed that you should be indifferent to death because it cannot be sensed. For them, fearing something that cannot be experienced was nonsense. Your Stoics, lead by Mr. Epictetus and Mr. Aurelius, proposed that mechanistic laws governing all natural phenomena determined your fate including death. They reasoned that if I brought you into this world then I can take you out therefore resistance to death is foolish. In their view, I determine the perfect whole, not you, circumstances you should accept. Some of your more recent thinkers like your Mr. Descartes attempted to understand death rationally. They thought you were two things-a mind and a body. This dualism enabled him to surmise that only your body dies and not your mind or soul which they thought was immortal. This last imaginary explanation particularly confounds you. You have wasted much time developing fanciful reasons to support this fanciful dualistic theory. All your explanations, however, are chimeras; you are trying to explain what for you is unexplainable.

The interesting question you should ask yourselves is why fear nothing? If you think about it you were nothing before you were born and you do not fear that, so why fear it after you die? I believe your Mr. Shakespeare said your little lives are *round with sleep*. You did not exist before you were born and had no sentience or experience. Essentially you were dead. So why suddenly be disturbed by this same state after you die? You face an odd contradiction here because on one hand you do not fear nothingness and lack of sentience and experience before you are born, yet on the other you do after you die. What changes? The answer is nothing. They are the same state and your fear is pointless. You being nothing is the rule and you living is the exception. Only your imagination makes you think living is the rule.

Practically speaking, your death is only fearful from your perspective. Why? If you must fear something, you have far more reason to fear living. Being alive is more dangerous and problematic than being dead. Living, unlike death, is dangerous and vexing. Further, living forever would truly be horrible. You would find the strain, effort, stress and anxiety unbearable for eternity. Besides, you would get bored. Once you had experienced all the good things life has to offer like movies, relationships, children, friends, meals, travel, conversation, love, work, books, sex and music you would have experienced them. They lose their novelty over time. Imagine, for example, that you could live 1,000 years. You would be utterly bored because you would have experienced everything, nothing would be new and you would just be doing the same old things over and over. Believe me, you would not like immortality. One of you said he looked forward to death precisely because it was his last great adventure.

In addition, the unpleasant things in life like hate, anger, revenge, poverty and sickness are happily erased by death. You no longer have to experience or endure them. This point makes conspicuous the idea that each of you views death a little differently because your perspective depends on the quality of your lives. If your lives are good then dying might naturally disappoint you. If, on the other hand, your lives are awful you might welcome it and feel relief. Your young, for example, tend to fear death more than your old do. When you are young and healthy death takes more than when you are old and feeble. For your old people death is often like an old friend who has come to extricate them from life's painful circumstances.

Ultimately, you think your death is significant because you think your lives are significant. Believe me when I tell you that both your lives and your deaths are insignificant. They are just pointless and meaningless events. It just does not matter if you die and it does not matter that it does not matter. It is a non-issue. Only your imagination makes it an issue. The truth is that your death would be something to fear only if you could survive it.

From my perspective, your death is no big deal. You and the other animals just come and go. The other animals do not mind coming and going, they accept it. It is just one of the patterns of nature. You, however, are anxious about the going. So how can I console you? Let me try to put things in a perspective you can understand. Ultimately, you do not go away and you do not become nothing. I know you are still there. You just rearrange yourselves as other parts of my patterns. You become parts of everything else. You become other people, animals, earth, rocks, air and water. You become rearranged. There is nothing evil or sinister or wrongful or fearful in being rearranged, it is just part of one large evolving process. If you can see this your deaths become far more intimate, acceptable and less fearful.

You were born to die. Your life's purpose is to survive and reproduce. To achieve this most of your lives are a hazardous advance through no man's land that ends in the valley of death. If you can just accept this and move on you will live more contented lives.

The Nature of Truth

If you think about it the nature of truth is your most significant question. It really involves three questions: does truth exist and if so, what is its nature, and can you know it? The answers to the first two questions are yes and it is that which is natural. It is that which occurs without interference from you imaginary metaphysical projections. Answering the third question is more difficult. You are capable of grasping bits of truth but usually do not recognize them when you see them. Your ken is limited which means that you can never entirely know truth. If you knew truth you would be omniscient and omnipotent, or me. I am giving you these observations in part to expose you to truth. This is my effort to explain what is true and set you straight on the true nature of things. Most of you undoubtedly will not accept my explanations, but I cannot do anything about that. It is simply a manifestation of your inability to grasp the nature of truth.

Your philosophers have spent considerable time debating this topic and have conceived of many inventive and creative explanations. All explanations, however, eventually fall into two categories: those that claim truth exists and those that do not. Most of your ancient philosophers, like Mr. Plato, believed in truth. He proposed a universal good and fixed truth. For example, he thought that certain forms were timeless and universal. Many contemporary philosophers have discarded any ultimate truth. Your Mr. Nietzsche, for example, denied any universal truth. He believed you created all truths. You create false opposites such as right or wrong and true or false that do not exist. He said these opposites assume an absolute truth which is a false assumption. Others, like your Mr. Sartre and his existentialist crowd, believed nature is essentially non-teleological. He thought your existence was random, meaningless, and without purpose.

But truth exists. It is all around you. Truth is the patterns of nature. It is your human nature and beauty. These are timeless and universal events. You know what truth is-you are truth and I am truth. The problem is that you are incapable of accepting these things for what they are. You are incapable of leaving well enough alone. You are compelled to impute meaning to things which gives rise to innumerable convoluted untruths. Truth also is often not pretty which bothers you. You want truth to be better than what it is so you endeavor to make it so. Because the patterns themselves offer no answers you use your imagination to provide answers. You create solutions and in the process utterly confound yourselves. The very word truth becomes baffling. The other animals have no such problem. They deal only in truth because they are not clever enough like you to deceive themselves. You are the only animal that deceives yourself which is one of the reasons I am taking the time to describe things to you the way they are.

The only reason you inquire about truth is because you imagination raises unanswerable questions about untruth. You get untruth when your imagination endeavors to alter the patterns of nature to improve what they offer. You do this a number of ways. You imagine constructs, ideas, ideals and concepts that are untrue and then wonder if they are true. These things create the opposites that Mr. Nietzsche discussed. When you declare one thing to be a certain way then you necessarily declare its opposite. If you had no construct of government, for example, there would be no anarchy; if you had no idea of morality there would be no immorality, and if you had not created an ideal like justice there would be no injustice.

Another example is your debate over free will and determinism. You wonder if your lives were determined or whether you had free will to change them. It was a silly debate set up by your theologians because they could not reconcile an omnibenevolent god in a world of evil. Let me just say your recent compatibilist philosophers with their common sense view that this is not about metaphysics but rather the freedom to act without arbitrary hindrance from other individuals or institutions is closer to the way it is. In nature it is determined you die but you have some choice over who your mate is and what you eat, just like the monkeys. Your cleverness creates the constructs that cause what is untrue which makes for untruth. These constructs naturally do not square with reality so you are forced into convoluted, anfractuous and sophistic reasoning to justify and make these untruths truths. You create artificial ideas which fragment and disturb my patterns and then twist logic to unify your knowledge. To put it plainly, truth is simple and you make it complex.

Your confusion over truth occurs because you misconstrue the nature of things and call things what they are not. You pass reality through your filter of self-interest and get not objective and true conclusions but rather subjective results that suit you. Your self-interest acts as a barrier to truth. The result is some very convoluted and wrongful ideas about the nature of things.

To make your untruths conform to reality you also confuse language and alter the very meaning of the word truth, a nasty habit that only perpetuates untruth. You give the word truth two meanings and unwittingly use them interchangeably. Earlier in this discussion I described big "T" and little "t" truth. Big "T" truth is timeless and universal and little "t" truth is personal and subjective. Big "T" truths are the patterns of nature and little "t" truths are your ideas, constructs, paradigms, social systems and imaginary concepts. These little "t" truths manifest themselves not only in religion but also in such things as your governmental systems, moralities and ideals. They are what you want to be true or what is true to you individually. They are not timeless and universal but rather temporary, changing and particular.

You have created a metaphysical mess with these two truths, a mess that causes you innumerable difficulties and much confusion.

Historically, you experienced big "T" truth by accident. Your art and philosophy projected ideas that sometimes were true. For example, they were true in art when you contemplated the beautiful and sometimes in philosophy when you used reason. These truths enabled you to experience and discover some of my patterns. But mostly, if you discovered a big "T" truth, it was accidental. Only recently have you begun rigorously applying your reason, mostly through science, and causing my patterns to increasingly reveal themselves. Unfortunately, these patterns will reveal only so much. They only give you glimpses when you get close to them. This is because, as I explained earlier, you are constitutionally incapable of knowing things-in-themselves, or big "T" truth. As your Mr. Kant wrote, you cannot understand the filters that enable you to make sense of the world; you can only see their consequences.

Time and Space

Of all your metaphysical speculations your interpretations of time and space are one of the most significant. These two concepts exert tremendous influence on your lives. How you perceive them determines much of your existence. I know this will sound fantastic to you but you cannot understand these concepts any more than you can know truth. You are incapable of comprehending them.

You are incapable of understanding what influences you. These concepts are like your parents, you know them but you do not. Your parents silently and unconsciously influence you in ways you are unaware. Like your parents you think you are independent of them but are not. Who you are, how you perceive things, what you do and your character and personality depend very much on them. Like your parents your interpretations of these concepts determine much of your existence. You are consigned to forever speculate metaphysically about the nature of time and space and what they mean. To explain this let me first describe your confusion, then why you cannot understand time and space, and finally how they influence you.

Your ideas of what constitutes time and space constantly change. Just read one of your science books to understand that your best and most imaginative thinkers cannot agree on what time and space mean. Your ancient Mr. Aristotle, Mr. Newton, and Mr. Einstein all disagreed. Mr. Aristotle and Mr. Newton thought time was absolute, separate and independent of space. With his theory of relativity Mr. Einstein disagreed and abandoned the idea of absolute time. He thought time was not separate from space but combined with it to form an object called space-time. Now you imagine a four-dimensional space and a curved or warped space-time. So what will your definition be tomorrow? You think you are getting closer to the true definitions of time and space but you never quite get there. You cannot get there because you cannot know them. Each of these thinkers disagreed because they could not know. They contemplated the properties of time and space through math and empirical investigation but not their natures. They endeavored to explain mechanics, not natures, which is like describing the mechanics of your automobiles without knowing what they are. Why? Because these concepts exist only in your clever little heads.

The reason you cannot understand the nature of time and space is difficult to explain. It is like attempting to explain the unexplainable, describe the indescribable, or teach quantum mechanics to squirrels. But let me just try to see where it takes us. Let me begin by referring to one of your thinkers, Mr. Kant. Every few hundred years one of you pops up and surprises me. I find myself thinking "How did that one figure that out on his own"? Your Mr. Kant is one of them. He came about as close as you can to explaining time and space. Although he used many confusing words he captured the essence of what I want to say. He said if you could look directly at reality, or things-in-themselves (that which is beyond your experience) you would not understand it. It would be unintelligible to you. You need something to make it understandable like an organizing filter. He figured this is what time and space do for you-they are the filters in your head that enable you to make sense of reality. What he discovered is that space and time are not things but rather forms of your internal sense or your way of understanding things. They are not independent of you but hard-wired into you. They are the way you apprehend things. He described them as forms of your sensibility. They are the parts of your natures that order experience which they do by spatializing and temporizing what you perceive with your senses. They are like *a priori* (before experience) filters that order experience.

What all this means is that your concepts of time and space are not real things but rather parts of your minds. In short, you supply time and space. Your mind imposes laws upon nature as both necessary and universal. You minds are not passive Tabula Rasas but rather active and creative entities ordering experience, reality and the universe. The beauty of Mr. Kant's revelation is that it allowed both scientific and synthetic *a priori* knowledge. This explanation may confuse you but it answers many of your questions and solves many of your problems. I was impressed.

The point in explaining all this is to show why you will never understand time and space. You cannot because they are the filters that make things understandable to you. These inborn filters arrange the world for you so what you are trying to describe is what you use to make sense of the world. You are trying to explain what explains things and describe what you use to describe. Put another way, you could not have an understanding of space and time without first having a concept of space and time, or as Mr. Kant so eloquently wrote, your thoughts without content are empty and your intuitions without concepts are blind. You will never understand time and space because you cannot explain them through deduction or abstraction which leaves only one method, your imagination.

As usual, your imagination steps in to fill your void of ignorance. Your imagination supplies the answers, you commence metaphysically wondering what they are and your problems begin. Because your imagination generates different meanings for these concepts you naturally disagree among yourselves what they mean, your ideas are constantly changing, you interpret them for selfish reasons, you politicize them and you misapply them. Your answers are always utilitarian in nature because your explanations are based on function and not truth. Most significantly, you begin using these concepts to justify and perpetuate your constructs. Naturally, the other animals do not have these problems because they are not clever like you. They do not question time and space but just use them to understand experience.

Originally, you had a limited conception of time and space. Your early people, in the case of time, made little distinction between the past, present and future. They lived in the present. But then your cleverness developed a sense of history and future which in your minds commenced a distinction between social, human-made time and the natural time of my patterns. Then your religious and governmental constructs began defining your futures and pasts for you. They promised you better futures and utopias. Because of your survival instinct you naturally seek security so these promises were appealing. But things got confusing for you when your different cultures began defining time and space differently. Your Mr. Rifkin observed how different cultures develop different concepts of time and space. In the case of time, he explained, your calendar cultures obtain meaning from the past while scheduling cultures obtain it from the future. The former is deterministic and stagnant and the latter believes in free will and improvement. The former follows traditions and the latter programs for the future. Then your religious constructs began interpreting time as the interval before your afterlife and therefore unimportant.

Your merchants then got in the game and interpreted time as a commodity which made it important and valuable. For them time was money. These differences exist because they each have different interpretations of time.

Consult one of your history books to observe how your perception of time and space has evolved and how they have changed you. Your concept of an hour, for example, did not exist in your early medieval societies. You did not invent it until the sixth century. But you wanted a further division so in the 1700s you used the pendulum to devise minutes. Because some of your cultures had concepts of hours and minutes and others did not some of you began imposing standardized time on everyone. You arbitrarily picked a place called Greenwich whose longitude would locate zero which established the basis for your world-time reckoning system. But you still were not satisfied, so with the help of your technology you invented more accurate clocks that measure seconds and computers that measure nanoseconds.

Your interpretation of space has also changed due to advances in your science and technology. Some of your older cultures perceive somewhere else as nowhere and many of the newer ones perceive nowhere as here. For some, the moon is sacred and spiritual and for others it is something to walk on. Now many of you wonder if you should be somewhere else and not where you are and others think you should be where you are and not somewhere else.

All this is significant because many of your concepts of time and space are increasingly incompatible with your nature which is disconnecting you from my patterns.

I created you to live within certain natural rhythms, such as the seasons, night and day, circadian cycles like eating and sleeping and the life cycles like youth and old age. But your concepts of time and space are changing all this. Your time is shorter and fast-it is no longer flowing and slow. Your concept of time increasingly means productivity, efficiency and wealth-it no longer means enjoyment. You no longer pass time, you spend it. Your concept of space is now international, infinite and unfamiliar-it is no longer local, immediate and intimate. Space is no longer comfortable but rather something to overcome and conquer. Many of you are no longer satisfied with where you are but only where you want to be. You are accelerating, disrupting and confusing your lives.

My point is this: you think your cleverness is bringing a better future with your evolving definitions of time and space but all you get are angst, unhappiness and disconnectedness. You are no longer relaxed and at peace. You find yourselves in a constant state of anxiety looking for better futures and environments. You find yourselves increasingly dissatisfied. Your lives are controlled by what no longer exists, the past, and what may never come in the future. Your imagination has detached you from nature's patterns and set you adrift on an existential sea of time and space. You are lost.

The Nature of Art

Your art surprised me. Originally, I thought it was just idle doodling on cave walls. You were bored so you doodled. You drew all sorts of things like animals, landscapes and other people. Your doodling pleased and entertained you. It was a luxury because you only did it when you had free time. Some of you claim that your art is not a luxury but a necessity. I assure you that it is not. You do it only after you have satisfied your other instincts. I believe your Mr. Adams once wrote:

> I must study politics and war, that my sons may have liberty to study mathematics and philosophy, geography, natural history and the naval architecture, navigation, commerce and agriculture, in order to give their children a right to study painting, poetry, music, architecture, statuary, tapestry and porcelain.

The other animals did not doodle because they were happily ignorant and satisfied with their circumstances. They did not need entertainment. But you doodled and much to my surprise your doodling progressed into something more than simple entertainment— it became productive. I noticed that some of your craftsmen began evolving into artists. You were originally craftsmen with an aptitude for making things. These things you knew and they were predictable. But then a few of them began attempting the impossible, creating new things and getting unpredictable results. Some evolved beyond craftsmen into artists and you invented the word genius. To my amazement, your artists began producing things outside my patterns of nature.

This development precipitated a flood of questions about art. Your Mr. Tolstoy asked, what is art? How was it to be defined? You began wondering what makes a work of art beautiful, appealing or ugly. Your Mr. Marx asked what the moral and social value of art was. You pondered whether your art was universal and essential. Some, like your Mr. Freud, wondered what role imagination had in your art You asked if it was heuristic. You contemplated the concepts of meaning, intention, representation and illusion in your art. You asked if it communicated things that could not be expressed other ways. This led to your most significant question: does art reveal truth or is it subjective? You raised more questions than you answered and in the process confused both of us.

To answer these questions you developed many theories about what your artists were doing. Your theories, however, were eclectic because your art is a vague thing. It is like a Tabula Rasa that lends itself to each individual's unique definition and interpretation. Some speculated that your art is pure imagination because you are the only animal who uses your imagination to tell stories. Some of you theorized that your art fulfilled an innate urge to understand yourselves and the universe. Others proposed that your art's importance was that it enabled you to share beliefs and values. It is essentially a cultural phenomenon. Many of you consider art primarily a creative process that makes connections between seemingly unrelated parts by recombining them. You developed innumerable additional ideas about art that emphasize things such as originality, tradition, style, self-expression, form and symbol. It is all these but much more.

The clue to your art's importance is found in your question: does art reveal truth? Is your art subjective or objective? It clearly is subjective. Fundamentally, your art is created to be liked rather than debated. This subjectivity is best seen in artistic aesthetics or that part of art that concerns the beautiful. Aesthetic artists perceive things through sensations, feelings and intuitions. It engages their values, tastes, feelings and attitudes about beauty that depend on many things such as familiarity, customs, habits and personal choice. Clearly, art expresses the feelings of the artist, communicates feeling and symbolizes feeling. Because each of these aspects affects individuals differently what is beautiful art varies from individual to individual and changes with time. This makes your art subjective.

But, to my surprise, art also has the potential to be objective, timeless and universal. It occasionally reveals truth. Your Mr. Plato and Mr. Aristotle were intensely concerned with this question of whether art could embody and communicate truth. It should not surprise you that your previously mentioned great thinker Mr. Kant, discovered the answer. He most ingeniously and unexpectedly explained it through aesthetics. He asked how judgments of beauty were possible. His idealistic philosophy explained that your cognitive powers constitute alike in the apprehension of the aesthetic whole or beauty. Judgments of what is beautiful express attitudes which themselves do not vary from person to person, and they are rooted in a disposition common to all, your human natures. It is a harmony of understanding by rational beings which contemplates and exposes my pattern of beauty. This consciousness of the harmony of understanding and imagination, which any rational being can feel, makes art objective. It also reveals truth because judgments of taste in beauty can be demanded of others. Interestingly and unexpectedly, this aesthetic consciousness of yours is one of the significant and unitary elements of all your experience.

Let me try to put it in simpler terms. Art is objective because you all universally and timelessly appreciate beauty. Art itself is not objective but you have a common ability to judge rationally and achieve a consensus that appreciates beauty. Put another way, what is beautiful pleases all of you universally and forever even though you may interpret it differently. This occurs because beautiful art mimics my patterns of nature, or beauty in nature. You have this ability in common because you have the same natural pattern within you. Art then communicates and connects this pattern or understanding regarding beauty which makes it an objective relation among you.

To this extent then your art is objective, timeless, and universal. It is objective because each of you knows beauty, timeless because your appreciation of beauty remains intact through time, and universal because each of you has the ability to appreciate beauty. Art is among the few mediums that uses your creativity to one universally understood end, which is beauty. What this means is that when you create beauty in art you are creating what you already know, which is beauty in art. This makes your history of art a record of your appreciation of beauty.

This brings us to the real importance of art: it uses your imagination to conceive future possibilities that go beyond my natural patterns. You forever want to be more than what you are. You perceive a greater potential for yourselves and art is one way you do it. Art is your cleverness and imagination working together to create new possibilities, things other than what is. If you did not imagine new possibilities you would never change. You imagined, for example, the possibility of a more survivable world, one without reality's limitations. Therefore, not only are sculptors and painters your artists but so are scientists and intellectuals. Artists are anybody using their imaginations to conceive of alternative future possibilities whatever they may be. Historically, your philosophers and painters were on the cutting edge of imagining these possibilities. Today scientists lead the way. Much of your futures today are imagined and achieved through your technology which is an extended art. Your computer programmers, for example, have become your cutting-edge artists because they conceive of programs that both imagine and enable your desired future possibilities. They were craftsmen but some became artists. These programmer artists are beginning to make those futures come true. It seems that you are art and your art is you. You are becoming many of those future possibilities that you imagined.

Unfortunately, your art has a downside. Some of those future possibilities are not true and many envision wrongful, even pernicious possibilities. Your artistic imagination sometimes goes metaphysically haywire. It sometimes takes you so far from the patterns that you endeavor to create impossible things and become things that you cannot be. Indeed, much of this discussion has been about your unnatural constructs which have caused you so many difficulties. One conspicuous example is your Mr. Marx who asked what the moral value of art was. He was an intellectual artist who envisioned a social collectivistic and communal possibility. It was to be a classless, property-less and atheistic society. It was to be a society where all individuals' material needs would be satisfied. This all sounded like a good possibility but it does not square with reality. When this new society did not naturally occur your Mr. Lenin brought it about by force and your Mr. Stalin killed those who resisted. Your art envisioned an impossible possibility and the consequence was many corpses.

One reason your art envisions wrongful possibilities is because it often communicates through metaphor, and as I discussed earlier, your metaphors are not always true. They enable you to make broad generalizations that sound good but are often vague and wrong. They sometimes express untruth. This sometimes makes your art a kind of literary bigotry. For example, to support his theory Mr. Marx said that metaphorically you were in chains everywhere. This is only a partial truth and partial truths have a way of being untrue. His metaphor was true to the extent that you do often chain yourself with your own constructs but it is untrue because the limitations in nature are inexorable. Mr. Marx made the metaphoric mistake of confusing your chains with nature's limits which caused him to imagine a partially true possibility. The consequences for you were just more artificial, self-created chains, to which Mr. Marx added a few links. These wrongful metaphors often send you into that metaphysical never-never land that causes you so many difficulties.

Science

For ages I was amused at your endless metaphysical speculations. You would imagine fantastic things and actually believe them. You imagined a flat earth and the sun circling your planet. But then, much to my surprise, you snuck up behind me and began figuring out my secrets. You realized that you were not getting anywhere with faith and that the stories spun by ancient others might not be true. So you began relying on reason and started discovering and understanding what I had done. You used your reason to create science, and in particular your scientific method.

It all started benignly. After observing my patterns you began theorizing. This did not catch my attention at the time because these theories looked very much like your other metaphysical stories. But then you did something different; you began assuming that you did not know and began testing your ideas. You would first observe, develop a hypothesis and then empirically experiment to test your hypothesis. If your hypothesis stood up you developed a theory which you then would test. You began practicing science and your cleverness became more help than hindrance.

This new method worked like a charm. Unlike your other metaphysical speculations it quickly began revealing my patterns of nature. It mimicked my patterns which you began reproducing in predictable and understandable ways. Your practical science began producing a cornucopia of benefits. Technology began generating useful things, psychology began exposing your essential human natures and sociology began uncovering the dynamics of your associations. You started approaching big "T" truth. This was a great achievement and I am impressed.

But this has been a blessing and a curse. You know the blessings. Electricity, medicine, cars, airplanes—the list is endless. They have improved your lives. But they have also brought many difficulties mainly because you began treating nature as a subordinate. Your Mr. Bacon, for example, exhorted you to torture nature so you could understand and conquer it. You now think you control my ways but what you will discover is that they control you. Needless to say, I do not appreciate this new attitude of yours. It is like saying you control the tiger by controlling its tail. You may have become adept at science but you have aroused the tiger and things are getting out of your control.

Unlike your social engineering my patterns of nature are like an equation, necessary and balanced on both sides. But this is a more dangerous equation than the one I described earlier. If you change one part of nature's equation another part necessarily changes and creates certain inexorable and often pernicious consequences. For example, you invent the internal combustion engine and get too much carbon monoxide, you create nuclear fusion and get plutonium (a very lethal entity indeed and one that is almost impossible to get rid of), you learn the cooling properties of Freon and end up destroying your ozone, you invent medicine and get overpopulation and you create computers and then think reality is punching keys. Before you were engaged in social engineering using your artificial constructs but now you are dealing with end things. Things not created by you, things beyond your control, things you will never fully understand and things that very likely may exterminate your species.

Recently, you have elevated your science to a deity and it is increasingly defining you. Previously, you had created ideas not only to understand what you could not explain but also to bring a sense of meaning and purpose to your worlds. Your explanations were teleological and laced with purpose. But your science does not offer meaning and purpose, it just explains. It does not explain the nature of things or tell you why they exist; it only describes what is. It does this because there is no meaning or purpose in nature; the patterns just are. Your science therefore is a strange mixture of convenience and big "T" truth that makes your existence increasingly barren.

Your science is beginning to upset my natural design. You are tinkering with the iceberg tip of nature and do not know how it affects the submerged part. This new ability to figure out and understand the patterns of nature has vastly magnified your ability to create and destroy. You now can exterminate your species at the touch of a button. You are playing with fire and you will get burned.

Philosophy

I love your philosophy. It is your effort to be me and I am flattered. The nature of philosophy, which is the love of wisdom, is your search for truth. As I mentioned previously if you could know truth you would be me. Your philosophy is your effort to think the way I think, see the way I see and know what I know. The patterns I created are necessary, unified and inexorable. They are perfect equations that you endeavor to understand with your philosophical and metaphysical imagination and more recently your reason. Your philosophy engages both your imagination and reason to generalize and unify your experience so you may comprehend my patterns.

My statement that your philosophy is the search for truth is no small thing. Your effort is profound and one that distinguishes you from the other animals. Your Mr. Plato wrote that philosophers are those "…who are lovers of the vision of truth." Your Mr. Spinoza wrote "Philosophy has no end in view save truth; faith looks for nothing but obedience." And your Mr. Leibniz claimed that he had always tried to uncover the truth. These are not trite statements. Down deep you want to know what is right, correct, accurate and true, and you disdain illusion, opinion and falsity. So you engage in philosophy and pursue truth in its broadest and most fundamental form. Many of your other disciplines also pursue truth but a more narrow kind. Your biology, for example, studies life but not what it means to live, your physics studies time and space but never questions the nature of matter, and your psychology studies behavior but never asks what the nature of emotions is. You can always ask what the philosophy of another discipline is but this is not reciprocal.

Your philosophy is unique because it explores truth in general and without limitation. Its very essence is to question everything to discover what is true. In its purest form it has no presuppositions. Your Mr. Descartes, for example, said he doubted in order to gain certain knowledge. Most of your problems are rooted in ignorance and philosophy is one way you overcome this ignorance. Truth does not readily reveal itself, especially when you are complacent. To overcome this your philosophers assume a posture similar to what your Mr. Sartre prescribed which is a perpetual state of quivering intellectual angst. This questioning state of uncertainty forces them to come to terms with their demons, illusions, denials and misconceptions because they are no longer comfortable. And in this philosophic state they commence questioning orthodoxy and approach truth.

Your philosophy, however, is a two-edged sword. It is one way you think yourselves into your metaphysical messes but it also is a way you think yourselves out of them. Philosophy is a hotbed of ideas where you create many of your constructs, ideals, paradigms and social systems that cause you the problems I have discussed in this discourse. But this philosophic search for truth is precisely what exposes their shortcomings. Generally, your ungrounded imagination causes most of your metaphysical Gordian knots. Your reason exposes them and your will, like your Alexander the Great, cuts them.

Your historic, philosophic search for truth involves a complicated equation consisting of experience, intuition and reason. It began with your awareness of sense experience that you interpreted with intuition. Like the other animals you originally just experienced things. Because this experience by itself made little sense to your clever minds you began evaluating experience with your intuitive metaphysical speculations.

You thought you could achieve truth by just thinking about it. You asked simple questions involving matter, change and yourself. These speculations remained unchecked for decades while they hardened into dogmatic orthodoxy. You became preoccupied with faith and your religion which dominated your philosophy for a long time. I often wondered if you were ever going to evolve beyond that stagnant phase.

But then to my surprise and pleasure you began to see the disconnect between what your Scholastics were preaching and the way things were. Intuition was not providing the answers you so desired. Your solution, unlike the other animals, was to use your reason. Many of your philosophers were instrumental in bringing about this change, but mostly Mr. Descartes held that truth derives from reason. He made a giant leap in your thinking but fell short because he discounted your knowledge gained from sense experience. You then took an intellectual detour when your Mr. Locke and Mr. Hume claimed that your knowledge was obtained only from experience. I watched with anticipation to see if you could work your way out of this dilemma which you did when your Mr. Kant synthesized these competing ideas. He proposed that you derive truth when both intuition and reason interpret experience. As you may recall, he pointed out that your thoughts without content were empty and your perceptions without concepts were blind. Voila! The door to true knowledge opened, your philosophy became more practical, you started a renaissance and you began doing things like science. Today you are reaping the practical and productive benefits of this revelation and have achieved a higher level of truth.

But, as I have said, you will never completely know truth because if you could you would be me. I am perfect and you are not which means in the end even your philosophy is limited. Ultimately, it will never answer your questions. Perhaps all that really can be said about your philosophy is that there is something exciting and romantically quixotic about your search for truth. Like your imaginary Mr. Don Quixote's vision of holding fast to the principle of righting all wrongs your philosophers courageously hold fast to the principle of attainting the truth in the face of convention. Even though ultimate truth is an impossible dream and just another windmill your search for truth in philosophy is its most enduring value. Keep up the good work. I am proud of you.

V

GOD'S CONCLUDING REMARKS

In light of my comments you could reasonably ask "Why not improve ourselves? Why not use our cleverness to make our lives better?" Certainly, you have demonstrated that you can improve my patterns of nature, so why not continue? Let me answer first by saying I understand and sympathize with your efforts to perpetuate your species and enhance your survivability. Your tenacious efforts to improve your circumstances have been remarkable and I admire your spirit of self-improvement. It is an irrepressible spirit that makes you special. The problem is that your efforts at self-improvement have a downside.

Because you can never know big "T" truth your imaginary constructs, ideas and ideals will never account for reality. Consequently, they too often create more problems than you started with. To make matters worse these new problems are often more serious than those you intended to solve. These new problems are the source of many of your maladies that torment and confuse you.

Just consider the problems that your constructs, ideas and ideals create for many of you. Most of you have great difficulty navigating these incredibly complex and artificial creations. Many of you lead confused, emotionally driven lives full of free-floating desire for money, sensual pleasure or prestige. These unfortunate souls are perpetually unhappy. You do not understand the nature of happiness, cannot solve the mysteries of life because you are superintended by intuitive passions and spend your lives pursuing false idols and defending false ideals. These ideals trap you in relationships and roles you cannot play. Most of you have been reduced to cogs in human-created huge, artificial societal machines. These machines control you, diminish your individual value and subject you to rules of conduct that are inimical to what you want. You find yourselves unable to communicate honestly with others because your language cannot adequately capture what your imagination has conceived. All the while you live illusionary lives because you cannot distinguish between what is true or false. No wonder most of you forever yearn for something better.

Clearly, the cleverest among you can navigate these imaginary labyrinths you created. But they are the lucky few. Consider the incredible difficulty your incompetents have maneuvering through what you have wrought. They are the less clever majority. They are ignorant, weak and have the least willpower. This unfortunate group cannot hold jobs, make enough money or keep their cars running. They live lives of quiet desperation utterly confused and constantly ridden with angst and unremitting fear.

The ultimate reason for all this is you are designed to exist within my patterns of nature. Outside them you will never be perfect. You may not like the truth but this is just the way it is. As hard as you may try your cleverness will never make you what you are not. The further your imagination takes you from the patterns of nature and the more abstruse your constructs become the more imperfect you will be. The further you endeavor to drag yourselves from your human natures the more you will find yourselves at war with yourself. And the harder you try to make concrete what your imagination has conceived the greater the danger you cause yourself. The more you endeavor to force your square peg constructs onto reality's round holes the bigger the mess. You have an inherent dilemma: the more you push the more nature pushes back, and nature bats last.

The best solutions I can give you, if they can be called that, are keep your imagination under control, especially your concept of amelioration, be grateful for what you have and appreciate love. You are not perfect outside my patterns and you only can do so much to improve your circumstances. When your solutions get too far from the patterns you encounter most of your problems. You need to stay close to the patterns, accommodate them, and mirror them. Do not fight them. You must keep your solutions simple and as close to your human natures a possible.

You also should appreciate what you have. You have a lot, far more than the other animals. Curiously, you are more inclined to be negative and count your curses than your blessings. You need to contain your desires because they are what inflame your imagination. They forever compel you to desire more. Appreciate what you have rather than what you have not. And finally, appreciate love. Most of you simply do not understand the value of love. It is a great gift. It makes you forget most of your problems and enables you to live in relative happiness and peace.

I will end my observations here. I have done my best to explain the way things are and how you have screwed things up. I hope you have learned something but I doubt it. I predict that you will persist in you ignorant, imaginary little worlds blaming me for all your problems. As I have repeatedly said, you are the problem and not me. I really have better things to do than spend my eternal life endeavoring to straighten out what you have done to yourselves. In the grand scheme you are a fruit fly with a 24-hour life, unimportant, insignificant and annoying. I am indifferent to your plight and wish you would stop bothering me with your irritating whining and complaints.

BOOKS BY JOHN L. BOWMAN

Reflections on Man and the Human Condition
Selected Topics in Philosophy
Nobody's Perfect
How to Succeed in Commercial Real Estate
Socialism in America
God's Lecture
A Reader's Companion
Stoicism, Enkrasia and Happiness
Aegean Summer
The Art of Volleyball Hitting
Graduate School
Provocative and Contemplative Quotations
On Law
A Reference Guide to Stoicism
A Reader's Companion II
Democracy
Philosophy and Happiness
My Travels (unpublished)
How to Get Rich
A Reader's Companion III
On Humans

www.ingramcontent.com/pod-product-compliance
Lightning Source LLC
Chambersburg PA
CBHW021952290426
44108CB00012B/1035